DISCOVERING YELLOWSTONE

An Introduction to the Park and its Ecosystem

By George B. Robinson

Introduction: Yellowstone is a place and an idea. Becoming the World's first national park in 1872, Yellowstone shaped the concept of protecting natural places for all future generations. **Page 3**

Geography: The park is geographically diverse and includes an area of about 3,468 square miles (8,980 km²) larger than Rhode Island and Delaware combined. **Page 7**

The Greater Yellowstone Ecosystem: This area maybe the largest, biologically richest and complex ecosystem in North America, outside of Alaska. **Page 46**

Wildlife: The richness and diversity of the fauna in Yellowstone offers a glimpse of pre-Columbian North America and a contrast to an increasingly fabricated world. **Page 51**

Geology: Influenced by what is called a hot spot, deep beneath the park, and shaped by huge volcanic explosions, the geology of Yellowstone is in constant motion, alive. **Page 19**

Ecology: From the lichen growing on rocks, to the mighty grizzly bear, everything in Yellowstone has its place. The rich diversity of plants and animals make this park unique. **Page 35**

History: The discovery of Yellowstone's wonders influenced the creation of what has been said to be "America's best idea": The creation of a national park system. **Page 67**

Yellowstone Quick Facts: The wonders of Yellowstone in facts and figures. General information about the park. How to further your research. **Page 80**

About the Author: Prior to his retirement in 1992, after ten years as Chief of Interpretation at Yellowstone National Park, George B. Robinson had a career in the National Park Service that spanned 32 years. He served in many areas including as Chief of Interpretation in Everglades National Park, Florida, and Wind Cave National Park, South Dakota. As one of the first professional interpretive planners stationed at the Harpers Ferry Center in West Virginia, George was involved in developing interpretive plans for several units of the National Park System, among them, Crater Lake National Park and Gulf Islands National Seashore. Since his retirement he has lived in Bozeman, Montana, with his wife Kae, and has continued to serve as a private consultant and freelance writer, calling his one-person firm *the wild side*.

Front Cover: The Midway Geyser Basin and the Firehole River. The Firehole River flows through the better known thermal areas of Yellowstone including the Upper, Midway, and Lower Geyser basins.
Photo by Laurence Parent

Left: Grand Prismatic Spring is the largest hot spring in the world. The amazing colors on its edges are produced by colonies of thermophilic microorganisms, which thrive at the different temperature ranges found in the spring.
Photo by Tom Till

Above: A large bison rests near Old Faithful in the Upper Geyser Basin on a cold morning. The thermal areas of Yellowstone provide welcome heat for wildlife during the coldest days of winter.
Photo by Dick Durrance

Designed and published by Elan Publishing, Inc. 2350 Commonwealth Drive, Suite E. Charlottesville, Virginia 22901. For distribution and ordering information please call: 1-800-284-6539. Join us online at www.Elanpublishing.com. Discovering Yellowstone © 2006 by Elan Publishing, Inc. All rights reserved. No part of this publication may be reproduced, stored in any retrieval system, or transmitted in any forms or by any means, without the written permission of the publisher.
All maps © International Mapping. All fish illustrations © Joseph R. Tomelleri. All other illustrations © W. Andrew Recher.
Library of Congress Catalog Number: 2005933584   ISBN Number: 0-9672957-3-4
Proudly designed and produced in the United States of America. Printed in Canada.

INTRODUCTION

Yellowstone! The word summons images of extraordinary things: ephemeral clouds of superheated steam rising above the leaden landscapes of geyser basins; sulfurous mud and water simmering in earthen vats; rivers falling abruptly into precipitous canyons; herds of elk and bison roaming freely through valley and forest; mountain peaks mirrored in the still, azure surface of a great lake; wolves announcing their presence in resonating howls; grizzly bears foraging for insects, pocket gophers, and wild berries; bighorn sheep climbing nearly perpendicular cliff sides; buried forests of petrified trees; massive, chalky-white terraces of travertine.

Yellowstone is also a celebration of the small, unspectacular and commonplace. Spawning cutthroat trout unerringly navigate small nameless tributary streams. Aquatic insects such as stoneflies and caddisflies are eaten in delicate or splashy trout attacks. Slime molds, essential to the decomposition and recycling of organic matter, grow on the forest floor. Red squirrels and Clark's nutcrackers harvest nuts from whitebark pines and cache them for future use. Hungry grizzly bears emerge from long winter sleeps and seek out these troves of food. Lichens form a living veneer that clings to bare alpine rocks where little else can grow. Mats of colorful microbes thrive in hot runoff channels from geysers and hot springs and harbor large numbers of tiny ephydrid flies. All this, and more, fashions a unique ecosystem that exists nowhere else in the world.

Beginning in the late 1860s, groups of residents of the Montana Territory entered the

"Stay on this good fire-mountain and spend the night among the stars. Watch their glorious bloom until dawn, and get one more baptism of light. Then, with fresh heart, go down to your work, and whatever your fate, under whatever ignorance or knowledge you may afterward chance to suffer, you will remember these fine, wild views, and look back with joy to your wonderings in the blessed old Yellowstone Wonderland."
from, Yellowstone National Park
by John Muir, 1898.

A bison stands outlined over the horizon.
Photo by Henry H. Holdsworth

Yellowstone region to see for themselves the many wonders described earlier by mountain men John Colter, Joe Meek, Jim Bridger, Osborne Russell, and others. Ferdinand V. Hayden, head of the U.S. Geological Survey, led an official exploration in 1871. Photographer William Henry Jackson and artists Henry W. Elliott and Thomas Moran accompanied Hayden. Members of these expeditions were so impressed with what they saw that they decided it should somehow be preserved for others to see and enjoy. Supported by the impressive imagery of Jackson, Moran, and Elliot, Hayden and others wooed Congress, urging its members to draft a bill protecting Yellowstone country for the benefit of everyone. Yellowstone became the world's first national park when President Ulysses S. Grant signed the bill on March 1, 1872.

Yellowstone is a place and an idea. The national park concept that took shape in the Yellowstone country became the model for 375 special places in America and the precursor to more than 3,600 parks, world biosphere reserves, and world heritage sites in 134 countries around the world.

Author Freeman Tilden, speaking of the national parks, observed that when Greek philosophers examined the world about them they decided that there were four elements: fire, air, water, and earth. Still, they believed that there must be something else, something intangible. If they could find it, there was a soul of things, a fifth essence, pure, eternal, and inclusive. Perhaps in Yellowstone you will discover it.

Left: A winter eruption of Old Faithful in the Upper Geyser Basin. Its name, coined by the Washburn Expedition of 1870, refers to its very regular eruptions. The strength of its eruptions is influenced by the power and duration of the previous eruptions and usually propel between 5,000 and 7,000 gallons (18,000 to 27,000 l) of superheated water as high as 185 feet (56 m) in the air. Their frequency, which can vary between 30 to 120 minutes apart, but are usually 45 to 90 minutes apart, are clearly predicted at the Old Faithful Information & Visitor Center.
Photo by Fred Hirschmann

Right: Symbol of wildness, the gray wolf was restored to Yellowstone in 1995 and 1996. Now more than 300 animals grouped in more than 30 packs populate the greater Yellowstone area. In the park, one of the best chances of viewing one of these powerful animals is in the Lamar Valley early and late in the day.
Photo by Joel Sartore

three

GEOGRAPHY

Yellowstone National Park is draped across the Continental Divide where Wyoming, Montana, and Idaho share common boundaries. It lies in the middle segment of the great Rocky Mountain cordillera, the mountain range that forms the backbone of western North America.

The park, almost all of which remains undeveloped, covers 3,468 square miles (8,980 km^2), larger than Rhode Island and Delaware combined. It sits on a high, volcanic plateau averaging about 8,000 feet (2,440 m) above sea level. Other federal lands surround and protect Yellowstone as part of what has been called the Greater Yellowstone Ecosystem. (See GYE chapter)

Yellowstone Country is geographically diverse. All of the classic elements of wilderness are here. The region includes: deep, icy-cold lakes; clear rivers, gentle cataracts, and thunderous cascades; high, barren mountains and forested plateaus; precipitous canyons stained by minerals; glacially rounded valleys and verdant meadows; steamy, sulfurous emanations from the underground; and abundant and diverse plants and animals. It is a place energized by a volcanic heart. There is no shortage of stunning features in this landscape. The Yellowstone region is characterized by high elevations, from the Reese Creek area, near the north entrance of the park, which is barely over one mile above sea level, to Eagle Peak, the highest in the park, which rises into the crisp, breathtaking air at 11,358 feet (3,460 m). Just beyond the southeastern boundary of the park, in the larger 28,000-square-mile (72,520 km^2) greater ecosystem, Gannett Peak towers to almost 14,000 feet (4,267 m). There is a great variety of relief in

A sign marking the crossing of the Yellowstone River at Fishing Bridge is partially buried by the deep snows of winter. Average snowfall in Yellowstone is 150 inches (3.8 m) but at the higher elevations of the park as much as 400 inches (10 m) of snow may accumulate. Yellowstone, and its greater ecosystem, including the surrounding national forests, are symbols of untrammeled wild America.
Photo by Jeff Henry

Yellowstone, with vertical differences between the base and summit of ranges typically of 5,000 to 7,000 feet (1,500 to 2,130 m). The landscape is covered by shallow, mostly volcanic soils, and harbors mineral wealth including vast deposits of gold, copper, silver, and even fossil fuels.

Most of the mountains of the Middle Rockies resemble the granitic upwarps of Colorado, but thrust faulting and volcanism have produced the varied and spectacular country included in Yellowstone. The Absaroka, Beartooth, and Gallatin ranges buttress the park on its eastern, northeastern, and northwestern margins. The Madison Range, Beartooth Plateau, Tetons, Centennials, Wind River, Washakie, and other ranges nested in the Middle Rockies lie beyond the park boundaries. Much of the outlying region is not mountainous at all but consists of extensive intermountain basins and plains, largely underlain with enormous volumes of sedimentary waste eroded from the mountains themselves.

The Absaroka Range, extending from northwestern Wyoming into Montana, along the eastern margin of the park and crossing portions of Gallatin, Shoshone, and Custer national forests, serves as a link between the Northern and Middle Rockies. The range is about 175 miles (280 km) long, and its highest point is Franks Peak, at 13,140 feet (4,005 m).

The Beartooth Mountains, just northeast of Yellowstone, are the highest range in Montana with numerous peaks higher than 12,000 feet (3,650 m). Their north face, called the Beartooth Front, is one of the most impressive mountain fronts in the Rockies. Their gradually rising high southern flank is referred to as the Beartooth Plateau and is accessible via

Preceding pages: The Lower Falls of the Yellowstone River in the Grand Canyon of the Yellowstone (see sidebar page 13). Falling about 308 feet (93 m), they are about 200 feet taller than the Upper Falls at 109 feet (33 m). Taken near Artist Point, South Rim.
Photo by Jeff Gnass

Left: The Kepler Cascades of the Firehole River drop more than 100 feet (30 m) in a series of small cascades. At this point the Firehole River cuts deep into the lava layers of the Madison Plateau. These cascades are easily viewed from a platform built near the road just south of the Old Faithful Village.
Photo by Carr Clifton

Right: The Yellowstone River flows through Hayden Valley following an ancient lake bed. The swampy valley, rich in grasslands and shrubs, attracts many animals from small rodents to large ungulates such as elk and bison, and provides a rich environment for waterfowl.
Photo by Laurence Parent

Geography

the Northeast Entrance of the park and the Beartooth Highway. Granite Peak, in the Beartooths, is the highest point in Montana at 12,799 feet (3,901 m). Within this range hundreds of alpine and sub-alpine lakes fill bedrock basins gouged out of the granite by glaciers.

The Gallatin Range is a 50-mile-long (80 km) section of the Middle Rocky Mountains in northwest Wyoming and southwest Montana. It rises to 10,967 (3,342 m) feet at Electric Peak above Mammoth Hot Springs. The Gallatin Range begins at Mount Holmes (10,336 feet; 3,150 m) in the Park and continues northward where it ends near Bozeman. The range consists of volcanic rocks originating in the Yellowstone Caldera. The topography consists of open ridges, steep 10,000-foot (3,000 m) peaks, deep remote drainages, open meadows, sagebrush slopes, and forests of Engelmann spruce, Douglas fir, subalpine fir, lodgepole pine, and whitebark pine.

The Teton Range, rising more than 7,000 feet (2,133 m) above the floor of Jackson Hole, is the product of uplift along the Teton Fault which began 9 million years ago. The Tetons' prominent features, south of Yellowstone, are among the youngest ranges in the Rocky Mountains. On a clear day, they may be seen from Avalanche Peak, Mount Washburn or other high vantage points of Yellowstone.

The Island Park Caldera, a broad plateau ringed by low hills, lies just beyond the southwestern park boundary west of the Madison Plateau. The Snake River Plain of southern Idaho lies beyond the Island Park plateau.

The Yellowstone-Absaroka region of northwestern Wyoming is a distinctive subdivision of the Middle Rockies. A large magma chamber beneath the area has filled several times and caused the surface to bulge, and to then empty in a series of volcanic eruptions of basaltic and rhyolitic lava and ash. Three such cycles have occurred in the past two million years, and about 640,000 years ago, the shape of Yellowstone was dramatically altered in an event that dominates its recent geologic history. The sudden release of more than 240 cubic miles (1,000 km³) of gas, molten rock, and ash in an explosion 1,000 times more powerful than the Mount Saint Helens eruption of 1980, produced an immense crater or caldera. Subsequent flows produced four prominent plateaus, forming much of the park's interior landscape.

The Pitchstone Plateau is a geologically young expanse of rhyolite lava, which flowed out of the caldera just 70,000 to 80,000 years ago. It forms much of the high ground beyond Shoshone Lake in the southwest quadrant of the park.

The Solfatara Plateau, named for its many fumaroles (or solfataras) is the product of a relatively small lava flow, which occurred about 105,000 years ago. It lies north of the road between Norris and Canyon Village.

The large Central Plateau, lies in the center of the park, entirely within the rim of the caldera and adjoining Yellowstone Lake. It was formed mainly by the Nez Perce lava flow, about 160,000 years ago.

The Madison Plateau, north of the Pitchstone Plateau, is the result of several lava flows of different ages. The road from the West Entrance to Old Faithful passes along its edges.

Four other elevated, extensive and relatively flat areas (the classic definition of a plateau), not formed by lava flows, lie wholly or partially within the park. Two Ocean Plateau is a high, rolling area averaging about 10,000 feet (3,048 m) above sea level, in the remote, and spectacularly beautiful Thorofare area south of Yellowstone Lake. Its name comes from an area, in the Bridger-Teton National Forest

---

THE CONTINENTAL DIVIDE

Rain. Snow. Ice. Runoff. High ground. In the simplified view of the reductionist, these would be the elements of the river cycle. Once freed from the clouds, water is pulled to the ground by the force of gravity and it is gravity again that drives the inexorable flow of runoff toward a distant ocean. But for gravity to move water, there must be high ground, whether a few inches or thousands of feet above the level of the sea, and high ground is the product of the work of geology. In this place, there is plenty of high ground.

On the Two Ocean Plateau, a small anonymous stream flows along the backbone of the country, the Continental Divide as it is called, then the water splits and becomes two streams dubbed Atlantic Creek and Pacific Creek. Slight changes in the streambed and changing water currents determine which way the water will flow, toward the southeast and the Gulf of Mexico through the Yellowstone River, or to the west and the Pacific Ocean via the Snake River. Isa Lake, between Old Faithful and West Thumb, lies perfectly centered on the Continental Divide. Water drains from one end toward the Pacific Ocean; from the other end it flows toward the Atlantic Ocean.

The Continental Divide marks the crest of a long series of mountain ranges that extend from Mexico through the western United States into Canada, the Rocky Mountain Cordillera. The Continental Divide is like the peaked roof of a house. Water falling on the divide flows east or west depending on which side it falls. Rivulets join to form small creeks, which merge into larger streams, which become rivers. Rivers gather the runoff and guide it unerringly toward either the Atlantic or Pacific oceans. The direction of water flow is determined by the diverse and rich topography along the divide, not a compass.

An often-confusing network of streams makes up a watershed. A good example of this is found at Madison Junction, where the south-flowing Gibbon River joins the north-flowing Firehole River to form the Madison River. The Madison flows west and then north to where it joins the Missouri River, which then flows east and then south to join the Mississippi River, which finally empties into the Gulf of Mexico.

The Yellowstone, Snake, and Green rivers are born in the Yellowstone high country. The Madison and the Gallatin rivers, two of the three forks that join to form the upper Missouri River, originate in the park. The Yellowstone River, the longest free-flowing river in the United States, also flows into the Missouri farther to the east. The Missouri joins the Mississippi, which eventually flows into the Atlantic Ocean in the Gulf of Mexico. The Snake River flows into the Columbia, which empties into the Pacific Ocean. The Green River flows generally south and joins the Colorado River, which eventually drains into the Pacific Ocean in the Gulf of California.

Yellowstone is hydrologically linked with both oceans because of the division of waters at the Continental Divide.

There is much water in Yellowstone and a visitor never seems to be far from flowing water or lakes and ponds. Of the 3,468 square miles (8,980 km²) of the park, more than five percent are covered by water, that's about 173 square miles (450 km²) distributed among more than 150 lakes and more than 500 streams. The streams alone crisscross the park with more than 2,650 miles (4,265 km) of flowing water!

(See dotted line on map at right)

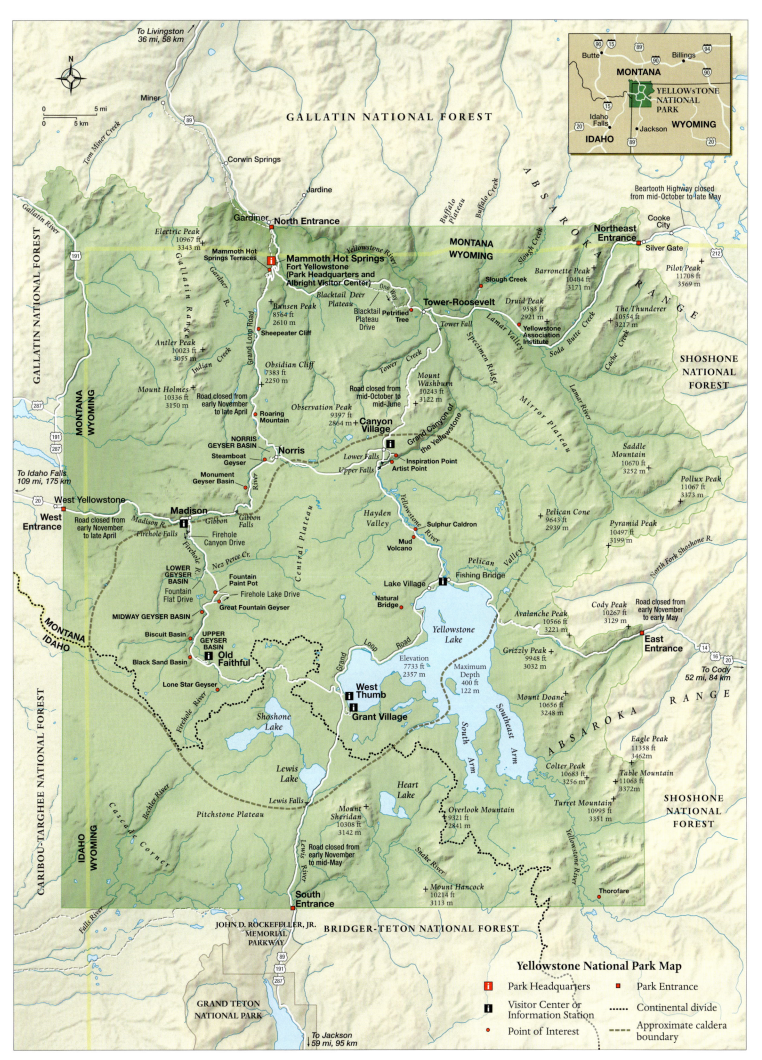

Geography

beyond the park boundary, from which streams flow toward both the Atlantic and the Pacific oceans. The headwaters of the Snake and the Yellowstone rivers are on opposite sides of the Continental Divide, near Two Ocean Pass. Historians think that mountain man Jim Bridger may have discovered the plateau in the early 19th century. The Mirror Plateau occupies much of the area between the Lamar and Yellowstone rivers in the northeast quadrant of the park. It averages about 9,000 feet (2,740 m) in elevation, and is named for Mirror Lake. Pelican Creek gathers runoff from the southern edge of

is characterized as cool temperate, with cold winters and relatively cool summers. The higher zone is alpine and tundra-like in character, with severe winter conditions and short, cold summers. Much of the total annual precipitation falls as snow in winter, although local, and sometimes severe, afternoon thunderstorms are common in the summer. Prevailing airflow is from the west, and eastern slopes receive less precipitation because of the "rain shadow" effect. Precipitation is highest in the southwest area of the park. Moisture-laden air, flowing in from the Snake River Plain, is lifted by the

the plateau and empties it into Yellowstone Lake near Fishing Bridge. The area surrounding this creek is one of the richest wildlife habitats in the park. The Buffalo Plateau, north of confluence of the Lamar and Yellowstone rivers near Tower Junction extends, into Gallatin National Forest. It was first seen and named by a group of prospectors in 1870. Its shallow grassy slopes were then, and remain, especially good bison habitat. Finally, the Blacktail Deer Plateau is an expanse of grassy, tree-covered glacial debris about 7,000 feet (2,130 m) high between Mammoth Hot Springs and Tower-Roosevelt.

The Weather and climate in the region are affected by latitude and elevation. Yellowstone is situated near the 45th parallel, halfway between the Equator and the North Pole, and its climate is influenced by the frequent passage of polar air masses. Because of its remoteness from any ocean, the area does not benefit from the moderating influences of these large bodies of water.

Precipitation increases with elevation while temperature declines. Two vertical zones prevail throughout much of the area. The lower

Continental Divide and drops 80 inches (203 cm) of moisture onto the Pitchstone Plateau. Predictably, lowest precipitation falls at lower elevations, about 10 to 12 inches (25-30 cm) near the north entrance. Precipitation in the remainder of the park varies with elevation.

Periodic droughts characterize the mountains and the intervening lowlands but long-term precipitation and temperature records, dating back to the 1870s, indicate no clear trend to wetter or drier environments. Temperatures have ranged from an historic low of 66 degrees below zero (-54°C) in mid-winter (recorded near West Yellowstone on February 9, 1933), to 98 degrees (36°C) in summer. In summer, it may be warm and sunny with temperatures in the high 70s, 80s or 90s (20s to upper 30s°C), yet, at night, the temperature may drop close to freezing (32°F, 0°C). The growing season is short, only one or two months in late spring, and some places are susceptible to frosts, even in summer.

Winter is a dominant factor in the life of Yellowstone. Temperatures often hover near 0°F (-17°C) throughout the day, but may reach highs in the 20s (-6 to -1°C). Subzero nighttime temperatures are common. Occasionally, warm "Chinook" winds lessen the chill by raising daytime temperatures into the 40s (5 to 10°C), causing significant melting of snow, especially at lower elevations. Annual snowfall averages near 150 inches (3.80 m) in most of the park. At higher elevations, 200 to 400 inches (5 to 10 m) of snowfall have been recorded.

Fifty percent of the annual total precipitation is held in the snowpack (the depth and density of accumulated snow) at the beginning of April, and is released to the soil and stream flow during the ensuing three months. There is insufficient rainfall to replace moisture lost by evaporation and transpiration (moisture loss from plant surfaces). If the snowpack is low, drought conditions can develop. Snowpack influences the habitats that ungulates feed in; their abilities to eat, travel and migrate; their vulnerability to predation; their expenditure of energy; and, it may determine which areas elk or wolves may occupy during winter. Snowpack also affects the timing and volume of stream runoff and plant production during the subsequent growing season. Lower than normal snowpack, coupled with regional precipitation and wind conditions, is a precursor to high fire danger in late summer.

Cold and snow often linger into April and May, although temperatures gradually climb with the advent of spring. Average daytime temperatures are generally in the 40s to 50s (5 to 10°C), reaching the 60s and 70s (15 to 21°C) by late May and June. Overnight temperatures frequently drop below freezing and may plunge near 0°F (-17°C). Storms in late May and early June may result in significant accumulations of snow with a snowfall of a foot (30 cm) in 24 hours not being uncommon.

Average maximum summer temperatures are usually in the 70s (20 to 26°C) and occasionally in the 80s (26 to 31°C) at lower elevations. Nights are cool, with evening temperatures sometimes in the 30s and 40s (-1 to 10°C). At higher elevations, temperatures may even fall into the 20s (-6 to -1°C) with a light freeze. Fall weather is generally pleasant, though cooler. Daytime temperatures average 10 to 20 degrees lower than summer with highs in the 40s to 60s

Above: The Yellowstone River, seen from Grizzly Point, meanders through the Hayden Valley. Herds of bison are often seen in this area. The Yellowstone River is the longest undammed river in the lower 48 states. Born in the Shoshone Range of Wyoming just southeast of the park, it flows to the Missouri River for a total of 671 miles (1070 km).
Photo by James Randklev

(4 to 15°C). Nighttime temperatures may reach into the teens and single digits. Snowstorms increase in frequency and intensity with the onset of winter.

In the mountains, changes in elevation bring changes in temperature, moisture, exposure to sunlight and even in soil quality, all of which affect the types of plants and animals that can thrive in different areas. Also, a more elevated and severe topography accelerates erosion and weathering. The greater the vertical relief the more obvious geologic changes become.

The lower elevations are predominantly treeless, except along

Geography

watercourses, where cottonwoods and other broad-leaved, deciduous species cluster into riparian habitats. Sagebrush steppe communities and grasslands typical of the drier northern plains occur in valleys and basins.

About five percent of the park is covered by cold water, most of it in the four big lakes nestled in the central plateau. Many times larger than the others, Yellowstone Lake is a dominant feature of the park. Shoshone Lake, Lewis Lake, and Heart Lake flank it on the southwest.

Yellowstone Lake is the largest, natural, high-elevation freshwater lake in North America. It is large enough to be easily seen from space. At an elevation of 7,733 feet (2,357 m) above the sea, its surface is 20 miles long by 14 miles wide (32 by 22 km) and covers 136 square miles (352 km²). The lake has 110 miles (176 km) of serpentine shoreline, joined by 124 tributaries. The deepest point in the lake is measured at 390 feet (120 m), and it has an average depth of 140 feet (42 m). In the geologic past the precursor to Yellowstone Lake was even larger. It was 200 feet (60 m) deeper and extended northward across Hayden Valley to the base of Mount Washburn.

Yellowstone Lake drains north through the Yellowstone River, but geologists believe that it originally flowed south into the Snake River. Today, the increasing size of a mass of molten rock beneath the northern lakeshore, called the Sour Creek Resurgent Dome by geologists, is gradually tilting the lake floor to the south so that its water may eventually flow again into the Snake River! Visitors in the distant future might find a dry and silent riverbed in the Grand Canyon of the Yellowstone.

The Yellowstone River is the last major undammed river in the lower 48 states, flowing 671 miles (1070 km) from its source southeast of Yellowstone National Park to the Missouri River. The river begins in the Absaroka Mountain Range on the slopes of Yount Peak, named for Harry Yount, believed to be the first Park Ranger in history, and flows through the spectacular Thorofare valley into Yellowstone Lake. It leaves the lake as a much larger river, and flows north over LeHardy Rapids, actually the true lake outlet, where it begins to meander peacefully through Hayden Valley.

At the north end of the valley, the river abruptly drops over the Upper and Lower Falls into the Grand Canyon of the Yellowstone and flows northeast to Tower Junction. There, freshened by water brought down from high in the Hoodoo Basin by the Lamar River, the Yellowstone tumbles through the Black Canyon, capped by impressive layers of columnar basalt. As the Yellowstone River leaves the park on its journey to the Missouri it is bolstered a final time with runoff collected by the Gardner River. On northwest slopes, the Gallatin River collects water, and drains out of the park, eventually

Above left: Mount Haynes towers at 8,235 feet (2,510 m) above the Madison River in winter. The Madison is born just east of this point at the confluence of the Gibbon and Firehole rivers. Flowing west out of the park it flows through Hebgen and Quake lakes and continues north where it meets with the waters of the Jefferson and Gallatin near Three Forks, MT, to form the Missouri River. Rich in trout population and the insects that feed them, the Madison is a world renown river for fishermen.
Photo by Jeff Henry

Left: The Hayden Valley under a deep cover of snow. The park's snow pack begins to accumulate in October and May depths might reach 400 inches! (10 m)
Photo by Jeff Vanuga

joining the Missouri at the confluence of the Madison and Jefferson Rivers.

The Snake River is the nation's fourth largest river, and the largest tributary of the Columbia River. It begins on Two Ocean Plateau and flows 42 miles (68 km) through the southern part of Yellowstone, where it is joined by the Lewis River near the South Entrance. It eventually adds Yellowstone water to the Columbia River and the Pacific Ocean.

On the west slope of Gannett Peak, nearly 14,000 feet high (4,267 m) in the Bridger-Teton National Forest, runoff is collected by the Green River. The Green flows south through Wyoming into Utah where it joins the Colorado River on its way to the Gulf of California.

Lying in the Snake River watershed east of Lewis Lake and south of Yellowstone Lake, Heart Lake was named sometime before 1871 for Hart Hunney, an early hunter. Other early explorers in the region incorrectly assumed that the lake's name was spelled "Heart" because of its shape, since then the spelling has persisted.

Shoshone Lake, the park's second largest lake, is located at the head of the Lewis River southwest of West Thumb. It is connected with smaller Lewis Lake by a short section of the Lewis River, which flows south, where it joins the Snake River. Fur trapper Jim Bridger may have visited this lake in 1833, and fellow trapper Osborne Russell certainly reached the lake in 1839.

There are 275 waterfalls, dropping 15 feet (4.50 m) or more and flowing year-round in Yellowstone. The highest waterfall, the Lower Falls of the Yellowstone River, is 308 feet (93 m). Tower Creek drops 132 feet (40 m) at Tower Fall, before joining the Yellowstone River. The Upper Falls of the Yellowstone River is 109 feet (33 m) high. Many of the waterfalls and cascades are located in the Bechler area in the southwest corner of the park.

Above: The Absaroka Range, formed by ancient volcanoes 53 to 44 million years ago, borders the park to the east. About 150 miles long, along the Wyoming-Montana border, most of the range is protected within Yellowstone National Park, the Absaroka-Beartooth Wilderness, the North Absaroka Wilderness, the Teton Wilderness, and the Washakie Wilderness areas. **Photo by Tim Fitzharris / Minden Pictures**

GRAND CANYON OF THE YELLOWSTONE

The Grand Canyon of the Yellowstone River is a striking incision in the landscape of the Yellowstone Plateau. The 19-mile-long (30 km) gorge is located in the north-central part of the park. The canyon is between 800 and 1,200 feet (240 to 365 m) deep and up to 4,000 feet (1,200 m) wide. It has brilliantly colored, red, orange and copper walls, mostly made of rhyolite from old lava flows. Here and there, touches of sulfur-yellow are added from still active geothermal features on the canyon floor.

The placid, slow-moving Yellowstone River abruptly tumbles over two spectacular waterfalls at the canyon's upper end. The Upper Falls drops 109 feet (33 m), and just downstream, the Lower Falls torrentially descends 308 feet (93 m), making it the tallest of nearly 300 waterfalls in the park. The volume of water flowing over the falls can vary from 63,500 gal/sec at peak runoff to 5,000 gal/sec in the fall. (240,000 to 18,920 l/sec.)

About 640,000 years ago, huge volcanic eruptions occurred in Yellowstone, emptying a large underground magma chamber. The cloud of incandescent gas and ash spread for thousands of square miles in a matter of minutes. The roof of this chamber collapsed, forming a giant smoldering crater several thousand feet deep. Following the collapse of the caldera, it was gradually filled by huge lava flows, one of which was called the Canyon Rhyolite Flow. The Canyon Flow came from the east and stopped just short of the present canyon.

A geothermal basin developed in this lava flow, and steam and gases emanating from the basin chemically and physically altered the rhyolitic rock. The usually hard, resistant rhyolite was softened and made more susceptible to weathering and erosion. Other lava flows, stemming from the caldera, blocked rivers and streams and formed lakes, including a large one in what is now Hayden Valley. The ancient lake overflowed and its waters cut through the weakened rhyolite, creating the canyon. Later the canyon was filled with glacial ice three successive times. Outwash floods, a product of sediment-rich lakes created by melting glaciers at the end of each glacial period, recarved and deepened the canyon.

The Lower Falls, the most spectacular, was formed where the leading edge of the Canyon Rhyolite Flow met the western edge of the old thermal basin. The hard cap of lava at the brink of the fall resisted erosion, while the softened lava in the thermal basin eroded easily. The Upper Falls was also formed at a contact point of hard and soft rhyolite lavas.

The canyon's general appearance today dates from when the last glaciers melted away. Since that time, water, wind, earthquakes, and other natural forces have continued to slowly carve and reshape the canyon.

Above: Upper Falls of the Yellowstone River drops 109 feet (33m) and was formed as softer volcanic rhyolite rock was eroded away.
Photo by Fred Hirschmann

thirteen

Geography

There are so many streams, cascades and falls that the area is also known as Cascade Corner. Twelve falls can be seen from the Bechler River Trail, and eight more are within easy reach. Among the most picturesque are: Terrace Falls, Union Falls, Cave Falls, Iris Falls, Dunanda Falls, Ouzel Falls, and Colonnade Falls.

Bechler River, Boundary Creek, and Falls River are the main watercourses draining the Pitchstone Plateau. They are tributaries of the Henry's Fork of the Snake River. The Bechler River was named after Gustavus R. Bechler, the chief topographer of the Hayden Expedition of 1872. This river begins at spectacular Three Rivers Junction, the confluence of the Phillips, Ferris, and Greggs Forks below Douglas Knob and the Continental Divide. Falls River rises on the Pitchstone Plateau and from Herring and Beula Lakes. This flow is joined by the Bechler River, giving it its name, above Cave Falls. Unlike most of the park, the Bechler River area has many large open meadows and boggy wetlands.

Hundreds of smaller lakes, streams, and cataracts, too many to list here, interconnect with their larger counterparts in a web of water that shrouds and nourishes the Yellowstone landscape.

Most of the park and its larger ecosystem are forested, and the vast majority of the tree growth consists of lodgepole pine, though there are other conifer species, as well as cottonwoods and aspens. Many types of wildflowers blossom in the warm months. In 1988 a massive series of wildfires temporarily altered large areas of the park, but natural restoration has been predictably rapid. The fires created a patchwork of new plant communities, adding to the already diverse flora, and stimulating changes in the fauna.

Animal life in Yellowstone is typical of the Rocky Mountains and includes 456 species of birds, mammals, fish, reptiles, and amphibians. And, true to the wild economy, where small things are of value, 12,000 species of insects and thousands of other invertebrates add to the fauna. Hundreds of different species of birds live in the park, among them many waterfowl, including the trumpeter swan. Trout is the most popular species with anglers, and the Yellowstone and other rivers are considered "blue ribbon" streams by anglers from around the world.

Yellowstone is a place of superlatives. The park contains half of the known geothermal features in the world, the largest concentration of geysers, and the world's tallest geyser. It is one of the few places in the world where travertine terraces like those at Mammoth Hot

Springs are found. The park also contains the world's largest petrified forest and the spectacular Grand Canyon of the Yellowstone. There are massive flows of rhyolitic lava, thick layers of columnar basalt, and a mountain of volcanic glass exposed at Obsidian Cliff. Native Americans are known to have quarried here to produce projectile points that have been found as far east as the Mississippi River.

Changes, from prodigious million-year-old geologic events, to the subtle ones that come with the equinox and solstice, make this an ephemeral landscape, a reminder that Yellowstone is a restless place; an unfinished painting. Like human history, both landscape and life are in a constant process of succession. In Yellowstone we see the remarkable ability of a natural system to recover, to restore dynamic equilibrium among its parts, to abide. Here, we can experience what it means for an animal to be truly wild, and be reminded that we share this place with organisms that have been on the planet far longer than we. Here, we see the ecological truth that complexity and diversity are necessary for the health and stability of natural systems. Yellowstone is geysers, canyons, waterfalls, and grizzly bears. It is diatoms, chipmunks, and smooth stones in a tiny stream. Yellowstone is the humbling lesson that we are merely guests in the house of nature, and that when she chooses to rearrange it, we can only stand aside, witness, and learn.

Most of the characteristic features of the park are accessible by road or trail. The park has more than 500 miles of roads and more than 1,000 miles of trails. The John D. Rockefeller, Jr., Memorial Parkway, an 80-mile scenic roadway that was established in 1972, connects Yellowstone with Grand Teton National Park to the south.

Visitors may enter the park from all points of the compass. The North Entrance to the park is at Gardiner, Montana, near the 100-year-old Roosevelt Arch that was rededicated on August 25, 2003 by Theodore Roosevelt IV. Visitors from the south enter the park via the John D. Rockefeller, Jr. Memorial Parkway. The West Entrance is located near the town of West Yellowstone, Montana. The West Entrance is the most popular, and is the quickest route to Old Faithful. The East Entrance is located about 50 miles (80 km) west of Cody, Wyoming. Folks entering the park by this route are encouraged to stop at the Buffalo Bill Historical Center in Cody. It includes the recently dedicated world-class Draper Museum of Natural History, which focuses on the Greater Yellowstone Ecosystem. The Northeast Entrance is located a few miles west of Cooke City, Montana. It is accessible via the spectacular Beartooth Highway, which climbs abruptly from Redlodge, Montana and crosses the alpine tundra of the Beartooth Plateau. A secondary, 26-mile-long road from Ashton, Idaho also reaches the Bechler River country.

Above left: View of Electric Peak (10,967 ft, 3,343 m), the highest peak in the Gallatin Range and the sixth tallest in Yellowstone.
Photo by Mary Liz Austin

Left: The Lewis River, named after Meriwether Lewis, has carved through the layers of lava and volcanic ash spewed out of the Yellowstone Caldera to form the Lewis River Canyon.
Photo by Carr Clifton

Above: The 84-foot high (25.6 m) Gibbon Falls tumbles over the edge of the Yellowstone Caldera. Much of the forest surrounding the falls was burned during the 1988 fires.
Photo by Jeff Vanuga

Right: Queen's Laundry hot spring in Sentinel Meadow on the Madison Plateau. This meadow was named in 1872 after the high geyserite mounds which stand as "sentinels" around this valley.
Photo by Jeff Foott

Geology

Geologic time is vast and geologic process, while sometimes occurring on a grand and spectacular scale, is often slow and imperceptible. Imagine a yearlong movie depicting just the last 750 million years or so of geologic history. If the movie started at midnight on December 31, a maturing Yellowstone landscape would not appear until late November, the first people would be seen early on the morning of December 31, and Yellowstone would be discovered, explored and established as the World's first National Park in the last couple of seconds.

Consider three volcanic eruptions that, in a matter of days, collectively ejected more than 900 cubic miles (3,750 km^3) of molten rock and incandescent ash, creating craters large enough to hold entire cities such as Philadelphia, Chicago, Denver, or San Francisco, with room to spare. Still, mountains are gradually carried away by the slow, subtle work of wind and water.

Rocks are the stuff of Yellowstone geology, and rocks are composed of minerals. If you were to examine a rock with a hand lens or magnifying glass, you would see that it is composed of a mosaic of interlocking particles that sometimes are big enough to be seen with the naked eye. These particles are minerals. Minerals are naturally occurring materials that have definite chemical compositions, and physical structures. Minerals are the geologic analogs to the cells that combine to form living organisms. There are hundreds of different types of minerals, each with its distinctive chemical composition and crystalline structure, but some are more common than others. Rocks mainly contain two or three principal mineral components, and while

Artemisia Geyser, named after the sagebrush plant (Artemisia tridentata) for its grey-green color, erupts as high as 30 feet (9 m) for a duration of 10 to 30 minutes and with intervals varying between 6 and 16 hours. It has the largest ornamented crater of all thermal features in the park, a large 55 x 60 foot (16 x 18 m) depression surrounded by a large formation of sinter. Sinter, also named geyserite and siliceous sinter, is formed as hot water travels through the underlying layers of rhyolite rich in silica. The heated water carries dissolved silica to the surface and, as it cools, deposits it in the form of sinter.
Photo by Jack Dykinga

Preceding pages: Steam from Excelsior Geyser and Grand Prismatic Spring rises over the Firehole River in the Midway Geyser Basin. The Grand Prismatic Spring is the largest hot spring in the park with a surface of about 250 by 350 feet! (75 by 100 m).
Photo by Tom Till

Left: The beauty of a sunset-colored sky over the frozen overflow of Castle Geyser. This large geyser, situated near Old Faithful, has a sinter cone about 12 feet (3.60 m) high with regular eruptions separated by intervals of 9 to 11 hours. Lasting up to an hour, these eruptions propel water about 60 to 90 feet (18 to 28 m) in the air.
Photo by Terry Donnelly

Right: Dawn at Mammoth Hot Springs. The waters brought to the surface at Mammoth carry a large amount of calcium carbonate, which is continually deposited to form the large terraces. These large deposits can grow at a rate of about two tons each day.
Photo by Charles Gurche

there are many mineral building blocks, there are fundamentally only three types of rocks — sedimentary, igneous and metamorphic — all of which are found in Yellowstone.

Granite is a coarse-grained igneous rock, solidified from magma, containing mainly quartz and feldspar, and smaller quantities of mica, hornblende, and other dark minerals. In Yellowstone, its pink color is due to high concentrations of potassium. This granite cooled slowly and solidified deep in the upper crust. Gneiss is a metamorphic rock with thick, dark-colored streaks. It is formed when older rocks, like granite, come into contact with superheated molten rock, or magma. Schist is a fine-grained metamorphic rock that contains many parallel grains of mica, a smooth, shiny, mineral that flakes into thin flexible pieces. Heat and pressure cause the crystalline structure and mineral composition of the original rock to change, or metamorphose. These are the oldest rocks in Yellowstone.

Yellowstone's basement rocks, what geologists call the ancient foundation on which the major geologic landforms are built, are very old pinkish, crystalline granites, dark-banded gneisses, and schists of the Precambrian era. That period of geologic time ended about 600 million years ago. These first Yellowstone rocks were uplifted and then large amounts of them were weathered and eroded away, completely removing pages from the geologic record. Some of the basement rocks are exposed in parts of the Madison and Absaroka ranges and extensive areas of the Beartooth Plateau.

Sediments deposited later, during the Paleozoic and Mesozoic eras, contain the fossilized

Geology

remains of organisms that lived in the shallow seas, swamps, rivers, and lakes that covered the region at different times. 500 million years ago, near the end of what geologists call the Cambrian period, the basement rock was covered by a shallow inland sea in which vast quantities of calcium carbonate, sand, and mud collected. These materials formed thick layers of sediment on the seafloor that would later become limestone, sandstone, and shale, all sedimentary rocks.

Then late in the Mesozoic era, a period of mountain building, geologists call it the Laramide Revolution, began as converging crustal plates forced up the Rocky Mountain region thus creating its chain of mountain ranges. That mountain-building episode, only a brief period in the geologic record, lasted from about 100 to 50 million years ago.

Following this uplift, erupting volcanoes began to build the Absaroka and Washburn mountain ranges that border Yellowstone on the east and west. The Absaroka and Washburn eruptions quit perhaps 40 million years ago, and were followed by a long period of uplift and erosion that continued until about 2.5 million years ago. A major volcanic period that shaped much of the landscape that we see today followed. It lasted until about 640,000 years ago, when some of the largest known volcanic eruptions in our planet's history took place.

It was during this cycle that a series of three massive volcanic eruptions, producing huge collapsed craters called calderas, shaped the Yellowstone Plateau and gave birth to Yellowstone's array of geothermal features. The eruptions were mostly of incandescent ash particles that were welded together by intense heat into a rock called welded tuff.

Those geologically recent events dwarfed the eruptions of Mount Mazama, Vesuvius, Krakatoa, Katmai, Mount St. Helens, and others that are usually listed as the largest. The most recent of the erup-

Above left: Giant Geyser was named by the Washburn Expedition because of the size and duration of its eruptions. Located in the Upper Geyser Basin, this massive cone geyser is about 12 feet (4 m) high with a diameter of about six feet (2 m) but its eruptions can reach a height of 150 to 250 feet (45-75 m). It has only erupted a few times since 1955.
Photo by Pat O'hara

Above: Heart Spring and the Lion Group of geysers including Lion, Lioness, Big, and Little Cub geysers. These geysers are interconnected under the ground and their cycles of eruption vary greatly. Lion Geyser has the largest cone and erupts in a series of 1 to 7, or more, discharges reaching 90 feet (27 m).
Photo by Tom Murphy

Left: Grand Geyser, in the Upper Geyser Basin, is a powerful fountain-type geyser with eruptions that can reach a height of 140 to 200 feet (42-60 m). The eruptions usually happen in a series of bursts, from 1 to 6, and have intervals that vary between 7 and 15 hours. Grand Geyser is the tallest predictable geyser in the world.
Photo by Jeff Foott

Calderas and Hot Spots

Yellowstone lies on a giant section of the earth's crust, what geologists call a tectonic plate, drifting with the other continents and seafloors on the hot, plastic mantle that encircles the earth. The North American Plate is a piece of a single primordial super-continent called Pangaea, which was dismembered by massive geological forces perhaps 300 million years ago.

Plate tectonics explains why chains of volcanoes mostly occur where the edges of constantly moving crustal plates are being subducted, or forced down into the mantle, by overriding adjoining plates moving in the opposite direction. These areas are the source of frequent earthquakes and volcanic eruptions.

The rise of volcanoes in the Yellowstone area began about 50 million years ago during a period of extensive mountain building as the western edge of the North American Plate overrode the eastern edge of the Pacific Plate. The Absaroka Mountains, which lie along the eastern side of Yellowstone, were formed during this period, which ended about 40 million years ago.

The shallow source of more recent volcanic activity in Yellowstone lies beneath the park. For decades a widely discussed theory about this "hot spot," far from the edges of intersecting continental plates, has been that it is the tip of a long-lived plume of molten rock extending deep into the mantle, perhaps to its base.

Theorists have maintained that as the North American Plate gradually drifted southwesterly over this stationary plume of magma it left the telltale path of older volcanoes and features extending from Yellowstone, through the Snake River Plain, toward the West Coast. Presumably, the older features passed over and were created by the same plume, like a welder's torch burning through the underside of the continent.

Through ongoing research, a new theory has recently emerged. It suggests that hotspots are not plumes from 1,750 miles (2816 km) or more deep in the mantle, as formerly thought, but arise from activity mainly in the top 120 miles (195 km) or so of the upper mantle. The new theory maintains that the upper mantle is much hotter and more fluid than previously thought, and that molten rock, or magma, is produced there by the release of pressure during the movement of the North American Plate. Advocates of the new theory believe that the insulating effect of the thick continental plate built up heat that eventually created the hot spot. The hot spot is traced back in time to a starting point near the edge of the continent.

While a technique called seismic tomography, which has been likened to a CAT-scan of the earth, discloses magma conduits similar to those predicted by plume theorists, they are only in the shallow mantle. There is no clear evidence of magma conduits below 250 or so miles (400 km) beneath Yellowstone.

Both theories acknowledge that the hot spot: generated massive volcanic eruptions that largely shaped Yellowstone; fuels the concentration of geysers, hot springs, and other geothermal features; and, left the series of volcanic footprints marking the landscape to the west.

About 16 million years ago, a series of huge volcanic eruptions began in what is now western Idaho and northern Nevada. The track of this volcanic activity neared present-day Yellowstone about 2.1 million years ago.

The volcano erupted under the southwestern portion of Yellowstone extending into the Island Park area of Idaho, creating a huge caldera, or basin-shaped crater. The volume of volcanic rock ejected by the first Yellowstone caldera eruption was about 600 cubic miles (2,500 km³), about 17 times more than Mount Tambora on the Indonesian Island Sumbawa and 2,400 times as much as Mount St. Helen's, and propelled ash as far as Iowa or Southern California! The collapse resulting from this volcano is called the Huckleberry Ridge Caldera. A smaller volcanic eruption, called the Henry's Fork Caldera, dated to 1.3 million years ago, occurred within the western edge of the Huckleberry Ridge Caldera.

More recent caldera explosions have destroyed much evidence of this event, but geologists can still trace many areas of the caldera rim. The yellow rocks in the Golden Gate area of northern Yellowstone, called welded tuff, are formed of ash from the Huckleberry Ridge eruption.

The next large volcanic event occurred 640,000 years ago. It was centered in what is now Yellowstone National Park, and resulted in the Lava Creek or Yellowstone Caldera. The caldera rim is still visible in many areas of the park, such as Gibbon Falls, Lewis Falls, and Lake Butte.

About 150,000 years ago, a volcanic explosion formed a smaller caldera within the southwestern rim of the Yellowstone Caldera. The West Thumb of Yellowstone Lake now fills it. Recent geological research has indicated near-surface volcanic activity on the floor of Yellowstone Lake, such as hydrothermal vents and uplifted, dome-like structures composed largely of silica. These features confirm that the magma plume which gave rise to the Yellowstone Caldera is still fueling the volcanic heart of Yellowstone.

The Yellowstone Caldera

Geologists believe that the hotspot that underlies Yellowstone has been burning up through the moving tectonic plate for at least 16.5 million years. As the North American tectonic plate moved gradually toward the southwest over the stationary hotspot, repeated eruptions left a track of 100 giant calderas (craters) across 500 miles (804 km) from the Nevada-Oregon border northeast to Idaho's Snake River Plain and into central Yellowstone. On topography and geology maps, the track of craters looks like giant volcanic footprints approaching the park.

Pressure from the growing chamber of mixed molten and solid rocks above the hotspot causes the Earth's surface to bulge upward and stretch outward. The crust fractures and cracks in a concentric or ring-fracture pattern.

Faults reach the deep magma chamber. Magma oozes through these cracks, releasing pressure within the chamber and allowing trapped gases to rapidly expand and erupt in a massive cloud of incandescent ash and gas.

With the venting of hundreds of cubic miles of pyroclastic material from the chamber, the surface no longer bulges. With nothing to support it, the roof collapses inward forming a huge steaming crater known as a caldera.

Subsequent to the collapse, over tens to hundreds of thousands of years, lava flows from within the caldera add great thicknesses of igneous rock, mostly rhyolite (fine grained volcanic form of granite), gradually filling the crater.

Still atop the hotspot, pressure, magma, movement of the heat, causes the Yellowstone caldera to inflate and deflate rapidly. This has caused two large bulges, called resurgent domes. The caldera floor is in constant motion.

Geology

Geothermal Features and Travertine Terraces

Yellowstone contains the largest concentration of geothermal features on the planet. Old Faithful Geyser is, no doubt, the most famous, but it is just one of 10,000 features known to exist in thermal basins scattered throughout the park. Yellowstone was designated a United Nations Biosphere Reserve in 1972 because of its unique geothermal features.

Geothermal features are formed by very hot water returning to the surface through a system of subterranean channels. There is plenty of heat and water, and millions of underground passages on this high volcanic plateau. Runoff from summer rainstorms, and melting winter snow replenish the ample water supply. Shallow molten rock, closer to the surface than in most other parts of the world, provides a constant source of heat. Gravity draws cold water down thousands of feet, through spaces in otherwise solid rock, where it collects, is heated to high temperature, and eventually returns to the surface as geysers, hot springs, fumaroles, mudpots, or travertine terraces. A web of fault lines and fractures, which form the geothermal plumbing system transporting the boiling water and steam, underlies the park.

Earthquakes, many only discernible by instruments and others big enough to be felt, are recorded almost daily. Larger tremors can make adjustments in the rocks underlying the park, altering the plumbing system, and in some case the frequency and intensity of geyser eruptions and the activity of other features. Geothermal features are sensitive indicators of underground movement and sometimes respond to earthquakes by stopping completely or reappearing in slightly different places. Occasionally earthquakes cause entirely new features to appear.

Above: Clepsydra Geyser is located off the Fountain Paint Pot loop walk, in the Lower Geyser Basin. This geyser always seems to be in eruption, but sometimes pauses when nearby Fountain Geyser erupts.
Photo by Tom Murphy

Right: The Norris Geyser Basin at sunset.
Photo by Tim Fitzharris

Geysers

As underground water is heated, temperatures rise well above the boiling point to 400°F (204°C) or more. Still, this deep superheated water remains liquid because of the great pressure and weight pushing down on it from overlying rock and water. As this water nears the surface in a constricted passageway in the rock, it begins to boil rapidly and bubbles upward. Steam eventually lifts the overlying water to the surface where it overflows, releasing pressure on the water column below. When pressure is released, deeper superheated water first flashes into steam and then erupts in noisy and showy displays. This temporarily empties the geyser until it is replenished with cool water, and the cycle repeats. All geysers are born of rock, water and heat, but no two are alike. They generally behave irregularly, but a few geysers erupt on schedule. Even Old Faithful sometimes changes its timing. Geysers such as Echinus Geyser in the Norris Geyser Basin are classified as fountain geysers. They spout water out in various directions through a pool. Castle Geyser, near Old faithful erupts in a jet of water from a cone-like formation. It is called a cone geyser. There are more than 300 known geysers in Yellowstone.

Hot Springs

Hot springs are the most common hydrothermal features in the park. Their plumbing systems are not constricted, so superheated water cools as it reaches the surface, sinks, and is then replaced by hotter water from below, just as air circulates in a room. This circulation pattern, called convection, keeps water from reaching the temperature needed to cause an eruption. Hot springs are located in all of the geyser basins and at Mammoth Hot Springs. They include Punch Bowl Spring in the Upper Geyser Basin; Grand Prismatic Spring in the Midway Geyser Basin; Silex Spring in the Lower Geyser Basin; Blue Funnel Spring at West Thumb; and Canary Spring which contributes to the travertine terraces at Mammoth Hot Springs. Hot springs are among the most colorful geothermal features in Yellowstone.

Photo by Fred Hirschmann

Fumaroles

Fumaroles or steam vents, are holes from which steam rushes into the air with a loud hissing sound. They are the hottest hydrothermal features in the park. There is so little water in fumaroles that it all flashes into steam before reaching the surface. Fumaroles are generally unspectacular and unnamed. They are distinguished by the particular noise that they make, and the rotten egg odor of hydrogen sulfide often associated with them. Two groups of note are Roaring Mountain north of Norris Geyser Basin, and Black Growler steam vents in the Norris Geyser Basin. Fumaroles may occur along tiny cracks or long fissures, in chaotic clusters or fields, and on surfaces of lava flows and thick deposits of pyroclastic flows. Fumaroles, like geysers, are manifestations of hot springs. They are also called solfataras.

Photo by Fred Hirschmann

Mudpots

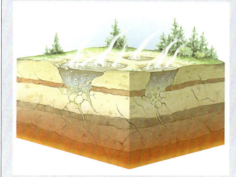

Mud Pots are acidic hot springs with a limited water supply. Heat-tolerant microbes use hydrogen sulfide gas rising from below as an energy source, converting it into sulfuric acid. The acid dissolves surrounding rocks into particles of silica and clay which mix with the small amounts of water to form a thick mud. Various gases, including some hydrogen sulfide, which cause a noticeable rotten egg odor, escape through the wet mud and cause it to bubble. Mud pots are curious, noisy, and odorous features, some of the most interesting are located south of Norris Geyser Basin at Artists' Paint Pots. Fountain Paint Pot, easily accessible, is a prominent feature in the Lower Geyser Basin. The Mud Volcano area, north of Fishing Bridge, boasts some of the most impressive boiling mud pots in the entire park.

Photo by Raymond K. Gehman

Travertine Terraces

The terraces at Mammoth Hot Springs are different from other geothermal features of Yellowstone as they are composed of travertine rather than sinter. Travertine is a material derived from limestone, a sedimentary rock composed of calcium carbonate, that underlies the area. As hot acidic water rises through the limestone, it dissolves large quantities of the rock and forms carbon dioxide. When carbonated water, carrying dissolved calcium carbonate, reaches the surface, some of the carbon dioxide escapes, depositing the white, chalky mineral called travertine. The terraces grow more rapidly than formations of sinter. Scientists have calculated that almost two tons of travertine are deposited each day on the visibly evolving terraces.

The terraces are also distinctive because they are located beyond the Yellowstone Caldera. Some geologists believe that the water of Mammoth Hot Springs flows along a fault line that more or less parallels the Norris to Mammoth road. Shallow circulation along this fault allows superheated water from Norris to cool to about 170°F (77°C), before coming to the surface at Mammoth. Ancient terraces extend from Mammoth Hot Springs down to the Gardner River.

Geology

tions produced an enormous volcanic crater in the center of the park. It is about 30 by 45 miles (48 by 72 km) in size.

granite, but it forms on the surface as thick, silica-rich lava cools. Often, it is ejected explosively in dense clouds of ash (welded tuff).

Less violent volcanic activity continued sporadically until about 70,000 years ago. During that time lava flows of reddish rhyolite occurred, partially refilling the caldera, forming much of the central plateau. Rhyolite is a volcanic rock that is the chemical equivalent of

A much smaller caldera eruption occurred during this period, about 150,000 years ago. It created a crater within a crater; the basin now occupied by the West Thumb arm of Yellowstone Lake.

More Recently, about 10,000 years ago, during a period called the Pleistocene epoch, or the Great Ice Age, glaciers began to form on the highlands. While the massive continental ice sheets of the Ice Age did not reach the Yellowstone region, the park lay under its own ice cap for thousands of years. The climate was much cooler then. Continuous snow fell and accumulated to great depths where it began to transform into glacial ice. Great ice sheets, as much as 4,000 feet

Above: Grotto Geyser in the Upper Geyser Basin, was named by the 1870 Washburn Expedition because of it unusual shape. It is believed that its dramatic cone, about 8 feet high (2.50 m) was formed by sinter covering fallen trees. Eruption intervals vary from 1 hour to as long as 2 days and can last from 3 hours to 13 hours. Since 1955, a transfer of thermal energy from Giant Geyser, just to the south, has accentuated Grotto's eruptions.
Photo by Jeff Foott

Left: Riverside Geyser was named by the Washburn Expedition for its location on the bank of the Firehole River. It has very regular and predictable eruptions with intervals of about 7 hours projecting water at a 70° angle over the river, sometimes spanning the entire Firehole River. With a powerful start, the eruptions can last for 20 minutes and end with a gushing of steam. It is a picturesque and popular geyser.
Photo by Jeff Gnass

deep (1,200 m) covered the park. Moving ice works on rock, just as a rasp and sandpaper work on wood. Mountain glaciers, moving slowly downward due to their own weight, carried abrasives that scoured and polished the maturing Yellowstone landscape.

Mountain glaciers flowed down valleys and out over the central plateau where they converged into a vast ice field that covered the whole region. During successive periods, ice flowed outward from immense ice fields, leaving behind U-shaped valleys, moraines, polished and striated rock, and huge boulders, called glacial erratics, dropped miles away from where they belonged. The Yellowstone

Ice Cap concealed even high mountaintops, which appeared as low mounds in a great sea of ice.

Yellowstone has experienced numerous periods of glaciation during the last two million years. Each glaciation destroyed most surface evidence of the previous glacial period, but scientists have found evidence of their history in sediment cores. It is believed that there were eight or more early glaciations in the Yellowstone region, but little is known about them. The Bull Lake and Pinedale glaciations are the most completely studied.

The Bull Lake glaciers covered the region about 140,000 years ago. They extended far to the south and west of the park, but no evidence of this glacial period is found to the north and east. Scientists believe that the forces of moving ice during the later Pinedale Glaciation erased evidence of the Bull Lake Glaciation.

The Pinedale glacial period began about 80,000 years ago and the last vestiges of its ice disappeared 14,000 years ago. At the peak of the Pinedale Glaciation, 25,000 years ago, nearly all of Yellowstone National Park was covered by a huge ice cap. The ice was 4,000 feet (1,200 m) thick above Yellowstone Lake. Mount Washburn and Mount Sheridan were both completely covered by ice. Geologists think that the Pinedale ice field occurred here, in

Above: The Fountain Paint Pot area is easily viewable in the Lower Geyser Basin. The rotten egg smells are a product of hydrogen sulfide gases filtering through the clay and silica forming the bubbles. Carbon dioxide also escapes and is part of the bubbling mix. The level of effervescence of this constantly growing area depends on the amount of ground water available.
Photo by David Muench

Above right: Great Fountain Geyser, situated along the Firehole Lake Drive is surrounded by one of the prettiest sinter deposits in the park. With predictable eruptions at intervals of about 10 to 12 hours, the waters of Great Fountain reach as high as 150 feet (45 m).
Photo by Londie G. Padelsky

Right: White Dome Geyser has a 20-foot high cone (6 m) sitting on a small mound of about 12 feet. Of a pinkish hue, due to deposits of manganese compounds, White Dome Geyser has unpredictable eruptions reaching 30 feet (9 m). It is also situated along the Firehole Lake Drive.
Photo by Charles Gurche

Geology

Geyser Basins

A few solitary features are located here and there, but most of Yellowstone's geysers are gathered into areas called basins. Most basins also contain fumaroles, hot springs, and some have mudpots. Upper, Midway, Lower, Norris, and West Thumb basins are all easily accessible by park roads. Lone Star, Shoshone, and Heart Lake basins are in the backcountry and require more time and effort to visit.

Geyser basins, discharging foul-smelling mud, water, and steam, look like open wounds in the forest. They are seemingly inhospitable places, which have developed near the rim of the Yellowstone (Lava Creek) Caldera. They are stark reminders that, while it is dormant, the Yellowstone volcano is still alive.

Geologists believe that the hot spot beneath Yellowstone caused the ground to swell upward, like a pie in an oven, and that ring fractures eventually developed around the edge. When the fractures reached molten rock, pressure was relieved, resulting in the eruption and collapse of the caldera. Geyser basins lie near where ring fractures have created conduits, allowing water to seep deep down toward hot rocks and then return.

Most of the distinctive geothermal landforms in geyser basins are formed by sinter, or geyserite. Sinter is an opalescent substance that is deposited by geysers and other thermal features. It is precipitated, on the surface, from hot water that has seeped upward through silica-rich (silica is quartz) rhyolitic rocks that cover much of the central plateau. The rate of deposition varies, but sinter is adding to geyser basin landscapes a few hundredths of an inch each year.

Geyser basins are usually colored by the gray of sinter, the yellow of sulphur, and the red, orange, and black of iron and arsenic compounds (in acidic features of Norris Geyser Basin and at Mud Volcano). Microbes that thrive in the hot environments of basins also add highlights to various features and runoff channels.

Water in all the basins has traveled several thousand feet down through openings in the rock, where the molten heart of the slumbering volcano heats it. Water temperatures underground are very high, 500°F (260°C) or more, and water and steam temperatures in the basins are often above 200°F (93°C). At elevations averaging above 7,000 feet (2,133 m) in the basins, water boils at about 199°F (92°C). Change is common in geyser basins. New features appear and old ones disappear. The eruptive cycles of geysers sometimes change. Some features are dormant for years, and unexpectedly come to life.

Upper Geyser Basin: Old Faithful Geyser is the most famous feature in the Upper Geyser Basin, but it is only the best known of many geysers. This Basin contains the largest concentration of geysers in the world, more than 150, but only covers about one square mile (2.5 km²). It is not the largest basin in the Yellowstone, that honor is claimed by Lower Geyser Basin to the north. The Upper Geyser Basin also contains many colorful hot springs. Black Sand Basin and Biscuit Basin, two smaller aggregations of features close to the Old Faithful area, are actually considered part of the Upper Geyser Basin.

Among the more famous neighbors of Old Faithful are Beehive, Grand, Giantess, Daisy and Castle geysers. Park naturalists fairly accurately predict the eruptions of some of these. Old Faithful jets straight upward in its unmistakable column of iridescent water and steam. The vent of Castle Geyser looks like a small medieval fortress. Riverside Geyser shoots sideways across the Firehole River. Grand Geyser erupts in a series of drum-like explosions. Punch Bowl Spring, with its low, scalloped edge, looks like a miniature caldera filled with a lake of boiling water.

Midway Geyser Basin: This basin appears to lie between the Upper and Lower Geyser basins along the Firehole River, but it is actually a small extension of the Lower Geyser Basin. It is the home of two of the largest geothermal features in the park. Grand Prismatic Spring, one of the most colorful and photogenic hot springs, is over 300 feet (90 m) across, and the largest hot spring in Yellowstone. Excelsior Geyser was the largest geyser in the world in the 1880s, but now it is just a large crater emitting lots of water. After 100 years of inactivity, it had some minor eruptions in 1984. Circle Pool, over 100 feet (30 m) across, and Flood Geyser are also located in Midway Basin.

Lower Geyser Basin: This basin is just south of Madison Junction. It covers close to 11 square miles (28 km²), and is the largest geyser basin in the area. Because of its size, thermal features tend to be scattered in widely spaced groups. Lower Geyser Basin is the home of Great Fountain Geyser, accessible by the Firehole Lake Drive, Imperial and Spray geysers near Fairy Falls, and the curious and odorous Fountain Paint Pot. Celestine Pool and Silex Spring and other features are accessible by a short boardwalk trail. The Lower Geyser Basin is the best place to see mudpots.

Norris Geyser Basin: Named for Philetus W. Norris, the second superintendent of Yellowstone, who provided the first detailed information about the thermal features, this basin includes three areas: Porcelain Basin, Back Basin, and One Hundred Springs Plain. Porcelain Basin is barren of trees, and its features are more concentrated. Back Basin is more heavily wooded with features scattered throughout. One Hundred Springs Plain is an off-trail section of the Norris Geyser Basin that is very acidic.

Norris sits above a busy subterranean intersection where earth-moving adjustments are continually being made. The Norris-Mammoth Corridor is a fault that runs from Norris north through Mammoth to near Gardiner, Montana. The Hebgen Lake fault runs from northwest of West Yellowstone, Montana, to Norris. These two faults intersect with a ring fracture formed during the collapse of the Yellowstone caldera. These faults are the primary reason that Norris Geyser Basin is so hot and dynamic. Norris is the hottest thermal basin, with a temperature of 459°F (237°C) at 1,087 feet (330 m) deep, and very few thermal features under the boiling point (199°F, 92°C, at this elevation).

Steamboat Geyser, the tallest, and possibly most unpredictable, geyser in the world is located at Norris. No other geyser is more indicative of the variability of eruptive cycles. Contrast its spectacular eruptions, from 300 to 400 feet high (100-130 m) and from 4 days to 50 years apart, with those of Bead Geyser (in the Lower Geyser Basin). Bead Geyser erupts 15 to 25 feet (4 to 7 m) in height every 23 to 30 minutes. Eruptions from Bead Geyser seldom vary more than 30 seconds from the average frequency. It is the most regular of all the geysers. While Old Faithful is the single feature most often associated with Yellowstone, it is neither the oldest, tallest, hottest, nor the most regular geyser.

West Thumb Geyser Basin: This basin is the largest geyser basin on the shores of Yellowstone Lake. The thermal features here are not just present on the surface, but also extend underwater. Scientists have discovered several underwater geysers. Their presence is indicated by smooth spots or slight bulges on the lake surface in summer. Black Pool and Abyss Pool are beautiful hot springs located in the West Thumb Basin. The West Thumb Geyser Basin, includes Potts Basin to the north.

part, because the hotspot beneath Yellowstone had pushed up the area to a higher elevation with colder temperatures and more precipitation than the surrounding land.

Evidence of the work of glaciers is found in many places. Especially good spots to see their eroding mark are the U-shaped valleys of the Lamar River and Soda Butte Creek, and near the Grand Canyon of the Yellowstone River. Also, near Inspiration Point, there is a huge, out-of-place granite boulder, a glacial erratic, encircled by pine trees. The house-size rock was plucked from the Beartooth Mountains by the grinding motion of an early Pinedale Glacier and dropped near the canyon almost 80,000 years ago.

Rock layers are subjected to continuous stress due to movement of tectonic plates. The layers sometimes bend and fold, but often the rock is weakened and cracks or faults develop. Faults are breaks in layers of rock involving horizontal or vertical movement, or both, along a line of weakness called a fault plane.

Earthquakes periodically occur along fault planes, as adjoining layers move against each other and tension is suddenly released. When this happens, waves of energy, called seismic waves, move through the surrounding rock, causing the ground to tremble.

Yellowstone is one of the most seismically active places in North America. Two thousand or more earthquakes occur each year in the park. Due to seismic activity and changes in the water supply underneath the basin, it is also the most changeable with new hot springs and geysers appearing frequently as others become dormant.
Photo by Jeff Foott

Left: Steamboat Geyser, located in the Norris Geyser Basin, is currently the world's tallest. With spectacular eruptions reaching 380 feet (115 m), and lasting up to 20 minutes, it is also one of the most unpredictable, with intervals of a few days to as long as 50 years.
Photo by Fred Hirschmann

Above: The Norris Geyser Basin, is the hottest and most acidic thermal basin of

Below: Fumaroles and hot vents in the Norris Geyser Basin.
Photo by Terry Donnelly

Geology

Hebgen Lake earthquake, with a 7.5 magnitude on the Richter scale, was the largest in the history of Montana. It caused a major landslide that buried many unsuspecting campers, dammed the Madison River, and created a new lake called Quake Lake. Seismic waves travel through solid and molten rock at different rates, just as sound moves through air and water differently. Geologists use seismographs and other instruments to develop images of the hotspot, and other geologic features underlying the park.

Following the uplift of the Rocky Mountains and the formation

the Yellowstone area. Most earthquakes are not discernible by people, but sensitive instruments called seismographs record even the slightest tremors, which often come in swarms. Earthquake intensity is measured on a scale of increasing magnitude, from one to ten, called the Richter scale.

Geologists identify two different kinds of seismic waves released by earthquakes. Primary waves travel quickly back and forth horizontally, compressing and stretching the rock. Secondary waves move up, down, and sideways through rock in a rolling motion. Earthquakes are felt when these waves reach the surface, causing the ground to move in a rolling or waving fashion. If the earthquake measures higher on the Richter scale, surface cracks, vertical displacement, and structural damage can occur. The 1959 Hebgen Lake and 1983 Borah Peak earthquakes were among the strongest in recent times. The

of the early Yellowstone landscape, eruptions from volcanoes in the Absaroka Range resulted in the accumulation of lava, ash, mudflows, and other volcanic debris, which buried large forests that had taken hold in the young, recently uplifted mountains. The trees of these forests, many of them standing upright, can be seen today as petrified or fossil forests.

Nearly 150 species of fossil plants have been discovered in Yellowstone.

Above left: Liberty Cap is a formation of travertine about 37 feet (11 m) in height. Formed by a spring which is no longer active, it is estimated to be at least 2,500 years old.
Photo by Terry Donnelly

Above: A male elk guards his harem during the fall rut at Mammoth Hot Springs.
Photo by Henry H. Holdsworth

Left: Dawn at Mammoth Hot Springs. Water seeping to the surface at Mammoth carries large amounts of calcium carbonate, which are continually deposited as travertine to form the large terraces. Ancient terraces extend down to the edge of the Gardner River.
Photo by Jack Dykinga

Right: Minerva Terrace is part of the Lower Terraces of Mammoth Hot Springs. Activity around these terraces changes daily with springs drying up and others coming to life.
Photo by Pat O'Hara

Geology

The great diversity of species in the fossil forests is an indication that the climate changed throughout the course of the area's history. The fossil forests include temperate, cool-climate species such as spruce, fir, and Sequoia, as well as laurel, magnolia, breadfruit, and even a relative of the mangrove, species found in warm, subtropical climates. There are also species such as walnut, oak, maple, and hickory, which are more typical of environments with moderate climates. It is not yet known whether layers of forests were fossilized where they grew, or if they were scattered before and after they were covered with debris.

Geologists believe that there were two chains of active volcanoes separated by a broad lowland, less than 1,000 feet above sea level. Subtropical and tropical trees flourished in the warmer valley and on its margins. The higher, colder slopes, rising 5,000 to 10,000 feet (1,500 to 3,000 m) above the valley, favored the growth of cool-climate trees like those found in the Yellowstone area today.

Animal fossils are also found in Yellowstone. Fossil invertebrates, including corals, bryozoans, brachiopods, trilobites, gastropods, and crinoids, are abundant in the limestones found in the northern and south-central parts of the park. Fossilized worm burrows have been found in some petrified tree bark.

Fewer vertebrate fossils have been found, but further exploration may uncover many more. Among the vertebrate remains that have been discovered are those of prehistoric fish, turtles, horses, bison, Titanotheres (a type of rhinoceros), and a marine vertebrate, which lived in a shallow inland sea more than 60 million years ago.

Episodes of crustal movement and volcanic activity have roughly shaped

Above: West Thumb Geyser Basin, here in a cold winter blanket of snow and ice, overlooks the beautiful Yellowstone Lake. A powerful volcanic explosion, about 150,000 years ago, shaped the West Thumb Caldera which later eroded and was filled with water, forming this area. There are few geysers here but this basin is dotted with hot pools and springs populated by thermophiles (heat loving microorganisms), responsible for their rich and marvelous colors. The thermal features of this basin also include the Thumb Paint Pots. Originally named "Mud Puffs" they include a series of small mud volcanoes surrounded by bubbling mud. The thermal features of this area do not end at the lakeshores but extend below the lake's waters. Wildlife, including bison and deer, can often be observed around this basin. The waters and shoreline of Yellowstone Lake provide a haven for many species of waterfowl.
Photo by Raymond K. Gehman

Left: Fishing Cone Geyser in the West Thumb Basin is a popular subject for photographers. The story was told by a member of the 1870 Washburn Expedition, that it was possible to fish from the cone, catch a trout, swing the fishing rod, dip the fish in the boiling water and cook it without ever unhooking it! Thus popularized, many tourists would have their pictures taken at what became known as the "Fish Pot" or "Chowder Pot." Because of many injuries to anglers and serious damage caused to the geyser structure, fishing or climbing on the cone is no longer allowed.
Photo by Larry Ulrich

the Yellowstone landscape: uplifting mountains; bending and folding layers of rock; spewing out lava and ash. Still, water and wind have always been at work through the processes of weathering and erosion, slowly and persistently adding cosmetic touches to the coarse landforms. Water, including glacial ice, and wind, work like fine sandpaper does on rough wood. They smooth and soften the contours of rock.

Weathering involves the disintegration or alteration of rock in its original position. Water and wind are its principal agents, although weathering can also be caused by chemical changes such as solution, oxidation and carbonation, and by living organisms such as by the action of expanding tree roots, or even by the dissolving actions of lichens.

Apparently solid rock is vulnerable to breakdown when it expands and contracts with changing temperatures. Water alternately freezing and thawing in cracks and fissures can pry layers of rock apart, a process called frost wedging. Dramatic variations in temperature cause intense freeze-thaw activity. As water freezes, its volume increases by about nine percent. If confined in rock fissures, it can exert pressures of about 29,000 pounds per square inch (2,038 kgf/cm²). This is enough to break the enclosing rock. Layers of rock often peel away from the surface in a process called exfoliation.

Weathered and unaltered rock is worn away, or eroded by the abrasive action of moving water and wind. The process of erosion includes the transportation of abraded and weathered material from the point of degradation, but not the deposition of material at a new site.

Sedimentary rocks are formed by the deposition and consolidation of particles of weathered and eroded rock or other materials. Over long periods of time, sediments consolidate, or lithify due to the weight of overlying layers and the cementing effect of minerals carried by water seeping through the layers. Sandstone and shale are common sedimentary rocks.

Sandstones and shales were deposited in inland seas that covered the Yellowstone region during the Paleozoic and Mesozoic eras, 570 million to 67 million years ago. They can be seen in the Gallatin Range and on Mount Everts, near the Mammoth Hot Springs area.

Wind and water-borne abrasives are at work right now behind the scenes, slowly wearing away hard rock and carrying pieces of Yellowstone to other places. Those sediments will, in the life cycle of stone, eventually form new rocks, which may become mountains again. According to nature's geological rules, what goes up eventually comes down. Old rocks become new rocks.

Above left: Petrified Trees of Specimen Ridge. This area is the largest concentration of standing petrified trees on the planet. Scientists have discovered more than seventeen forests buried here. The process of petrification began as the trees were buried in volcanic matter and mudflows. The wood slowly turned into stone when minerals, dissolved in water, seeped into the tree fibers and later solidified. The trees were left uncovered as erosion cleared the surrounding softer materials.
Photo by Jeff Foott

Above right: The basalt columns at Sheepeater Cliffs were formed by the rapid cooling of lava flows. As it cooled and shrunk, the lava cracked in these polygon-shaped columns in what is called "columnar jointing."
Photo by Willard Clay

Right: Fields of erratics left strewn about in the upper Lamar Valley. These rocks were carried for miles by long-gone glaciers which deposited them here.
Photo by Willard Clay

Ecology

Ecology is defined as:
1: a branch of science concerned with the inter-relationship of organisms and their environments.
2: the totality or pattern of relations between organisms and their environment.

These Lichen covered rocks and alpine flowers are as much a part of Yellowstone as the popular geysers and grizzly bears. They are part of a whole, defining the richness and diversity of the Greater Yellowstone Ecosystem, where all parts are as important as the next and should be protected.
Photo by Art Wolfe

Definition by permission from the Merriam-Webster Online Dictionary © 2005 by Merriam-Webster, Inc. (www.Merriam-Webster.com)

Preceding pages: Midway Geyser Basin is probably one of the more scenic thermal areas of Yellowstone. The Firehole River meandering through this basin, as well as the Upper and Lower Geyser basins, collects runoffs from many geysers and hot springs. By the time the Firehole reaches Firehole Falls, below the Lower Geyser Basin, its temperature has been raised by about 59 degrees F (15 °C).
Photo by Laurence Parent

Left: Winter scene of lodgepole pine at Black Sand Spring. The lodgepole pine, named for its use by Native Americans in the construction of their shelters because of its slender and straight trunks, is the most widely distributed conifer in the park and in the Intermountain West.
Photo by Fred Hirschmann

Right: Misty forest of lodgepole pines and high grasses. Yellowstone harbors more than 1,700 species of native vascular plants, 170 species of non-native plants, and 186 species of lichen.
Photo by Jeff Foott

As populations of plants and animals interact with one another, they form what are called biological communities. The term biodiversity refers to the number of species and individual organisms in these communities, and the complexity of their relationships. In nature, diversity and complexity are healthy conditions. Research has shown that species rich communities are able to recover faster from disturbances than species-poor communities, a fact well illustrated by Yellowstone's dramatic recovery from the epic fires of 1988.

Regardless of the diversity of organisms, or their place in the ecosystem, fundamental relationships are much the same, and are governed by general precepts that bind everything together into an ecological whole. The connections of living things with their environments, and with one another, are myriad. Some are simple; others are complex. All of them involve exchanges of air, nutrients, and energy.

Plants are the producers of the food that nourishes and sustains the animal life of the Greater Yellowstone Ecosystem (GYE). They capture solar energy through the process of photosynthesis and absorb nutrients from the soil and water. During the long, harsh winters, conifers retain their needles, which extends their ability to photosynthesize. Deciduous trees like aspens and cottonwoods contain chlorophyll in their bark, enabling them to photosynthesize before they produce leaves. During photosynthesis, stores of nutrients in plant tissues become available to consumers as food.

Food is passed from herbivores (plant eaters) to carnivores (meat eaters), which are in

turn consumed by larger carnivores. Grass becomes flesh and bone; the mosquito becomes the damselfly; the damselfly becomes the trout; the trout becomes the bear. The sequence in which energy and nutrients pass from producers through successive levels of consumers is known as a food chain, and each stage in the transfer of energy is called a trophic level. At each level of assimilation in this process, energy is lost as heat and to the metabolic processes of the organisms involved. Food chains combine into larger more complex patterns, called food webs.

Grazing food chains involve consumption of living matter. Consumers of dead matter are part of detrital food chains. Some microbes are part of food chains in which dissolved organic matter is consumed. A typical grazing food chain in Yellowstone could include, algae fed on by mosquito larvae, which in turn are eaten by trout. The trout then becomes food for a pelican, otter, bear, or a hungry angler.

Detrital food chains are most common in natural systems where less than ten percent of the primary production is grazed. In such a system, substantial and complex buildups of biomass, the total weight of living matter in a given area, can occur, increasing energy storage in the system. A typical detrital food chain in Yellowstone could begin with dead plant material, eaten by bacteria and fungi, which are consumed by single-celled animals. Worms and insects eat the protozoans, and are then consumed by birds.

The relationship of numbers and size of organisms in a food chain is depicted graphically

thirty five

as a pyramid of numbers. From bottom to top of the pyramid, the numbers decrease, and the size of the organisms increases. The greatest amount of energy available is in the green plants, the primary producers, at the base of the pyramid, with successive levels of consumers (primary, secondary, tertiary) above them. The higher the organism is on the trophic pyramid, the less energy is available to it.

Solar heat and light flow through and energize the entire system, except in the dark throats of geysers and hot springs. In nearly every functioning ecosystem the ultimate source of energy is and dying organisms such as slime molds and bacteria), based on whether they are plant eaters, meat eaters, both, or decomposers.

Nutrients, elements and inorganic compounds that are essential to life, are circulated through the GYE in what are called material cycles. The hydrologic cycle is perhaps the best known. It involves the perpetual circulation of water through evapotranspiration, the combination of evaporation and transpiration, or water loss from plants, condensation, and precipitation. In addition to the water cycle, other material cycles that circulate nitrogen, phosphorous, sulfur, and carbon through the system are important.

the sun. There are self-nourishing organisms, called autotrophs or producers, which convert and concentrate the solar energy into food. Consumers or heterotrophs are animals and even certain plants, such as bladderworts, which utilize, rearrange, and decompose material made by the producers. Decomposers are the link between death and new life.

The main energy source for producers is sunlight and the indirect energy of air and water required for photosynthesis. Another unusual source of energy production is sulfur-oxidizing bacteria, called chemoautotrophs, which thrive in the hot, sulfur-rich waters of geothermal features.

The primary energy source for consumers is food, a direct or indirect product of photosynthesis. Consumers are designated as herbivores (elk, deer, bison, and other ungulates), carnivores (wolves, bobcats, mountain lions), omnivores (grizzly bears, black bears, people), or saprovores (microorganisms that consume dead

One of the best ways to visualize these, and other interrelationships in the GYE, is to think of the ecosystem as a living organism. Air and water are its metaphoric breath and blood; carbon, nitrogen, phosphorous, and other compounds are its foods, which if not properly balanced can cause illness. Green plants and air breathing animals, including people, are the lungs of the ecosystem. The sun energizes the movement of air, water, and nutrients through the ecosystem. Energy is transferred in the GYE and its life forms, through various ecological relationships that connect everything like arteries and veins in a complex circulatory system.

Ecological processes are continuous, one blending almost imperceptibly into the next. Still, plants are the foundation on which all other living systems in the GYE are built, and there is a great variety of plant life in many plant communities carpeting the once-barren volcanic landscape.

Over 80 percent of the park is forested with eight species of conifers (cone-bearing evergreens), but mainly with lodgepole pine. Grasslands cover about 15 percent of the area. Engelmann spruce, Douglas fir, sub-alpine fir, juniper, aspen, and cottonwood are common. At higher altitudes, the venerable whitebark pine endures high winds and low temperatures. Sometimes, after centuries of growth, it becomes a spreading tree, gnarled, and thick at the base. There are over 1,700 species of vascular plants, more than 120 species are rare, ranging from those of the desert to ones adapted to the alpine tundra. Common plants in the park include: big sagebrush, heartleaf arnica, yampa, goldenrod, globe huckleberry, elk sedge, mountain snowberry, and serviceberry. Unfortunately, more than 170 species of exotic or non-native plants have taken hold in the park. They are hardy, aggressive plants that can out-compete native plants for water and nutrients. Efforts are underway to exclude them.

An increase of 1,000 feet (300 m) in elevation is roughly equivalent to moving 300 miles (485 km) closer to the North Pole. Environmental conditions in Yellowstone vary from near desert to arctic tundra. Elevation ranges from 5,282 feet (1,600 m) at Reese Creek near Gardiner, Montana, to 11,358 feet (3,460 m) on the summit of Eagle Peak in the Absaroka Range. Differences in temperature and precipitation that accompany changes in altitude and latitude, (Yellowstone lies near 45° north latitude), can cause changes in vegetation and the animal life associated with plant communities. In addition, plant cover changes in response to the composition of soils.

Alpine tundra is supported in areas above 10,000 feet (3,000 m). About 90 percent of the structure in some plants is in the roots storing nutrients and energy during poor growing periods. Flowers are often large but other plant parts are small to save energy and reduce exposure to the rigors of the wind and cold. Most of the plants are slow-growing perennials. Short, stocky trees give way upslope and on extremely windy ridges to bare fields (fell fields) with sparse, low-growing vegetation and scattered boulders covered with lichen. Moss campion, mountain avens, native dandelions, and others are among the few plants that

Above: A small herd of bison roams free in the Midway Geyser Basin. The bison herd of Yellowstone are descendants of the original local herd mixed with animals that were transplanted from other areas of the country. Although larger concentrations are seen in the Lamar and Hayden Valleys, the bison can be seen in nearly every part of the park. They are large animals, standing about 6 feet at the shoulders and weighing up to 2,000 lbs. (900 kg) for an adult male or bull.
Photo by James Randklev

can survive in the high, harsh environment. Plants often grow very close to the ground, and above the thinning forest at timberline, twisted, contorted, and deformed shrub-size trees grow. They are called krummholz a German word that means "elfin timber," or "crooked wood."

Lichens grow in all of the communities, ranging from orange-colored, elegant sunburst lichens clinging to alpine boulders, to green, beard-like, stag horn lichen draped from pine boughs. Lichens are

Ecology

BEYOND THE NAKED EYE

Geothermal features are on the opposite end of the size spectrum from large systems such as the Greater Yellowstone, but similar bioecological processes are at work. The often sunless, scalding worlds of geysers and hot springs are miniature, albeit very stressful,

ecosystems. Because the conditions that exist in its geyser basins are thought to be similar to those on the primordial earth, heat-tolerant microorganisms that dwell in the vents and runoff channels of Yellowstone's thermal features are helping scientists envision how life might have begun on our planet.

Scientists, led by Microbiologist Thomas D. Brock, professor emeritus at the University of Wisconsin-Madison, have discovered one-celled organisms living in the scalding environments of boiling springs and geyser vents. Since the mid-1960s, Dr. Brock has done field research in Yellowstone and has carried out a wide range of studies on the biology and geochemistry of the park's thermal systems. Brock's discovery of some of these microscopic life forms has become the basis of a 500 million dollar industry that has led to the first bioprospecting agreement ever entered into between Yellowstone National Park and the private sector.

Visitors generally associate big animals such as bears, elk, and moose with Yellowstone. Yet, organisms with some of the greatest economic and scientific impact on our world are invisible to the naked eye. They can only be seen when they form filaments and dense mat-like layers. The heat-tolerant organisms that live in and near Yellowstone's thermal features have been dubbed "thermophiles" ("thermo" for heat and "phile" for lover). They are so tiny that a 3"x3" (10 x 10 cm) mat contains as many thermophilic microorganisms as there are people on Earth!

Microbiologists have learned that the organisms thriving in Yellowstone's thermal features contain enzymes that are stable at extreme temperatures. These properties were discovered to have major implications for research in medicine and technology. An enzyme from the bacterium *Thermus aquaticus*, discovered by Dr. Brock near the Great Fountain Geyser area of the Lower Geyser Basin, was used in the late 1980s to make *taq polymerase*, a key ingredient in a laboratory process called the polymerase chain reaction, or PCR. This process, making it possible to copy and amplify DNA, helped science in the field of medical diagnosis, in evolutionary studies when DNA is present in fossils, and in forensic science, where it is essential to the process of DNA fingerprinting. This process was so important to science that its inventor, Kary B. Mullis, was awarded the 1993 Nobel Prize in chemistry.

Important industrial applications are also based on some of these bacterial components. The bacterium *Thermoanaerobacter ethanolicus*

Above left: Little Whirlygig Geyser, at Norris Geyser Basin. The green mats on the edge of the runoff channels are due to the presence of photosynthetic algae and the presence of green chlorophyll.
Photo by Larry Ulrich

Above: Hot spring algae patterns in the Biscuit Geyser Basin.
Photo by Jeff Foott/Larry Ulrich Stock

Left: Hot runoffs from the Grand Prismatic Spring flow into the Firehole River. The striking colors are due to the pigments present in different heat-tolerant microorganisms called thermophiles. Their discovery and application in the scientific field are responsible for a thriving industry. It's a reminder of what Henry David Thoreau said: "the little things in life are as interesting as the big ones."
Photo by Jack Dykinga

produces enzymes that are used in the conversion of waste product cellulose into ethanol. A form of ethanol called gasohol has been used as energy efficient alternative fuel.

Bacteria, algae, cyanobacteria and primitive organisms called Archaea, once considered a type of bacteria, are also responsible for the colors in thermal runoff channels and on the edges of hot springs and other features. They thrive at different temperatures and carry different pigments, so they function like colorful thermometers. Organisms that use light as a source of energy contain green chlorophyll as their pigment and are called photosynthetic. They thrive in cooler temperatures away from the main features at the edges of runoff channels and are composed of algae and bacteria known as cyanobacteria. The other microorganisms present in and around the features, called non-photosynthetic, contain pigments called carotenoids and are found in the hottest part of the features. These pigments are responsible for the red, orange, and yellow colors.

In general, and remembering that colors and the appearances of pigments can be affected by the intensity of sunlight, colors in the hottest waters in and near the features (180°F and higher; 82°C) are usually pale yellow and pinkish-white. The colors turn to brighter yellows when the temperature drops to about 160°F (71°C). Orange becomes the dominant color when the water cools to about 145°F (62°C). Browns and greens are the main colors at temperatures of 120°F (48°C) and lower.

The chemistry of hydrothermal pools also affects the kinds and abundance of life present in their waters. Archaea grow in alkaline hot water, although some, such as *Sulfolobus acidocalderius*, are also found in acidic environments. They are found in features such as Octopus Spring and Obsidian Pool in the Lower Geyser Basin. In cooler, acidic features in the Norris Geyser Basin and the Mud Volcano area, the algae *Cyanidium* forms neon green mats, while *Zygogonium* adds the purple color. The cyanobacterium *Phormidium* forms an orange mat in neutral areas such as the runoff channels of Castle Geyser and Grand Prismatic Spring. Another cyanobacterium *Synechococcus* and the bacterium *Chloroflexus* grow in yellow and yellow-green mats and *Calothrix*, a cyanobacterium, appears brown in cool, neutral runoff.

Above: The deep blue areas of Grand Prismatic Spring are too hot to support any of the microorganisms that add color to its outer edges. The deep blue is sunlight scattered and reflected by water particles and molecules, as in most bodies of water.
Photo by Raymond K. Gehman

Below: The colorful appearance of Morning Glory Pool varies according to the seasons. At its hottest it appears bright blue, as the seasons turn cooler, it turns green, yellow, and even brown.
Photo by Jeff Foott/Larry Ulrich Stock

Ecology

cooperative alliances between fungi and algae. The alga uses sunlight to make sugars as food for itself and the fungus. The fungus provides protection from environmental stress such as excess light. Lichens are one of the best examples of symbiosis, relationships among species in which there is mutual benefit to both organisms. If lichens growing on a boulder are examined with a hand lens, they look like miniature coral reefs, and one scientist has called them "the forests of Lilliput." There are 186 identified species of lichens.

The spruce-fir zone, situated above 8,400 feet (2,560 m), is dominated by stands of spruce and fir interspersed with lodgepole pine and whitebark pine, growing in andesitic soil or receiving more than 40 inches (1 m) of precipitation each year, or both.

The lodgepole pine zone, between 7,600 and 8,400 feet (2,300 to 2,560 m), is dominated by even-aged lodgepole pine with occasional spruce, fir, and whitebark pine. It receives 20 to 40 inches (.5 to 1m) of precipitation annually, and is underlain mostly by rhyolite.

The Douglas-fir zone, between 6,000 and 7,600 feet (1,800 to 2,300 m), is dominated by Douglas-fir occasionally interspersed with, aspen, and lodgepole pine, but big sagebrush and various grasses cover more area than forest. This zone lies along the Yellowstone and Lamar River valleys. Less than 20 inches (50 cm) of rain falls here each year. Various depths of glacial till, derived from the granites and andesites upstream, underlie the zone. There are occasional outcrops of limestone in the valley, which may add calcium to the till.

The riparian zones, narrow ribbons of forested land that border creeks and rivers, represent only a small percentage of the region, but they provide essential habitat for many animals. Along their lower courses, cottonwood and willow trees are common.

A small area along the northern boundary of the park is much drier and has a vegetation type similar to that found throughout the Great Basin. With less than 15 inches (38 cm) of precipitation each year, it

Above: Nez Perce Creek meanders through a forest of lodgepole pine trees, from Yellowstone's Central Plateau to the Lower Geyser Basin where it joins the Firehole River. This creek is named after the dissident Nez Perce Indian tribe which, in 1877, under the leadership of Chief Joseph, fled from incarceration in reservations through Yellowstone, on their hopeful journey to Canada.
Photo by Adam Jones

Below: Yellowstone Lake is the largest natural high elevation lake in the country. Situated at an elevation of 7,732 feet (2,400 m) it has a shoreline of 110 miles (176 km) joined by 124 tributary streams. It measures about 20 miles (32 km) in length and 14 miles (22 km) in width to cover 136 square miles (352 km^2) to an average depth of 140 feet (42 m). Its deepest point is 390 feet (120 m).
Photo by James Randklev

is composed of saltbush, greasewood, winterfat, blue gramma, and other species. The heavy sedimentary soils are derived from shale.

Hayden Valley and Pelican Valley are largely treeless, but well covered with grassland species. Both areas are ancient lakebeds from the Ice Age and are covered by thick deposits of lake sediment. This probably accounts for the treeless condition.

The many different plant communities are classified according to habitat and cover type. Habitat type describes the sets of environmental conditions conducive to the growth of specific groups of plants. Cover type describes the successional stages through which a plant community passes following a major disturbance such as a large fire, infestation of mountain pine beetles, or a period of glaciation.

Plant succession is an orderly, and predictable sequence of plant communities occupying a site following a disturbance. Depending on the extent of the disturbance, some species may survive; other species may be restored from nearby habitats; and others may actually be released from a dormant condition by the disturbance. Each new disturbance within a landscape creates an opportunity for a new species to colonize that region. New species also alter the character of the community, creating conditions that favor even newer species. Such cyclic disturbances occur periodically in Nature. For example, fire ecologist believe that large scale wildfires will sweep through old growth lodgepole pine forests in the park every 300 years or so.

At every stage each plant species has characteristics that adapt it to the soil, moisture, nutrient, lighting and other conditions of the site. The process begins with the earliest, or pioneer community, and continues until little change in species composition occurs, a condition known as the climax community. As the forest develops, the environment changes, and new plants and animals become more abundant.

Soon after a fire (or other event) in Yellowstone, spectacular regrowth begins. Pioneering herbs and shrubs take hold on the forest floor. Colorful displays of fireweed, heartleaf arnica, wild strawberry, dandelion, leafy aster and elk sedge flourish. Aspen shoots and millions of lodgepole pine seedlings sprout through the altered soil. Pioneer species are well adapted to an open, sunny environment where there is little competition for water and nutrients.

In mid-succession, lodgepole pines mature, and species such as Engelmann spruce and subalpine fir are scattered about the under-

Above: A flight of Canada geese over the Yellowstone River. The riparian communities in Yellowstone offer a vital refuge for countless species of plants and animals providing food, water, shade, shelter, cover, and important nesting sites. As in other parts of the country, they are the most productive and vital areas of the landscape.
Photo by Jeff Henry

Ecology

WILDFIRES: FUEL, HEAT AND OXYGEN

Fuel, heat and oxygen, elements of what fire ecologists call the fire triangle, occasionally combine, under the right conditions, to create wildland fires that burn in Yellowstone's forests and grasslands. Ecologists know that fire has been an important element in the natural processes of the entire Greater Yellowstone Ecosystem. Fire is within the group memory of plant and animal populations, which have inhabited this area since the Ice Age.

Lodgepole pine, which forms nearly 80 percent of the forest in the park, is a species that requires the intense heat of a fire to release seeds from a portion of its cones. Lodgepole pines produce two types of cones: one that opens at maturity and a slow developing, or serotinous, type that opens only after it has been heated. The serotinous cones ensure a ready seed source for seedling establishment after a fire.

Records indicate that an average of 22 small to moderate-sized fires are started each year in Yellowstone by lightning. Fire-scarred Douglas-fir trees in the Lamar Valley indicate an average frequency of one fire every 25 to 60 years in that area. Large fires are known to have swept through Yellowstone in the 1700s, and are believed to reoccur every 300 to 400 years on average.

Still, until the late summer of 1988, no large fires in recent memory had visited the mostly even-aged, forest of lodgepole pine. Ecologists refer to such a forest as an old-growth monoculture, which is an ecologically unhealthy situation due to the lack of species diversity.

From the time of the park's establishment in 1872 until 1972, a policy of full fire suppression was in effect as forest fires were viewed as destructive and dangerous to all public lands, their structures, and to the public. In 1972, the National Park Service began a managed fire program that acknowledged the natural role of fire. This approach allowed fires to burn naturally if there was no threat to human life or property. Yet, during the ensuing 16 years only a little more than 34,000 acres (13,800 ha) burned.

What made the summer of 1988 so unique was the product of many years of fuel accumulation, the driest summer on record, and a succession of dry cold fronts adding strong winds to the mix. As lightning-caused fires started the fire season in late May, they were allowed to burn according to the park's policy. By then there were no signs of the drama to unfold as some fires went out naturally and others continued to be monitored.

As the summer progressed and the drought worsened, small fires began to grow and quickly merged with larger ones, and by the end of July more than 99,000 acres (40,000 ha) were ablaze. By then the park officials had begun an all out war to suppress the expanding fires and local firefighters were joined by teams of firefighters and military units from across the country. Strong winds, whipping the blaze, carried embers across firelines and streams, causing the fires to spread during the whole month of August.

On August 20 alone, more than 150,000 acres (60,000 ha) burned, pushed by strong winds. The fires reached a most dramatic point on September 7, when one of the larger fires, the North Fork Fire, jumped the Old Faithful area, burning some 20 cabins and outbuildings and more than 100,000 acres (40,000 ha). It seemed that the entire park was ablaze.

Finally on September 11, the first snows fell on the park and succeeded in dampening the fires. The firefighting effort now had the upper hand.

More than 790,000 acres (3,200 km²) of forest in the park, and many thousands more acres in the surrounding area had burned during a period of about three months representing about 36 percent of the total acreage of the park.

The firefighting effort was unprecedented with more than 25,000 firefight-

Above left: Flames crown-out during the firestorm near Grant Village, during the historic fires of the summer of 1988. Nearly 50 different fires started during that summer but only a few massive complex fires were responsible for the great majority of the nearly 800,000 acres (3,237 km²) that burned.
Photo by Raymond K. Gehman

Above: Regrowth following the fires of 1988, and other small fires since, can be seen throughout the park.
Photo by Art Wolfe

Left: Hearleaf arnica carpets the floor of the coniferous forest burned on Mt. Washburn during the 1988 fires.
Photo by Jack Dykinga

ers and military personnel joining in the fight at a cost of over $120 Million.

Although cataclysmic in appearance, the fire actually cleansed and invigorated the system by reducing the old-growth forest, opening the canopy, and releasing nutrients, so that more vibrant pioneer plant species could begin the process of succession again. The fire created thousands of miles of biologically rich community edges, where plant and animal species from adjoining communities merge in what is called an ecotone.

Following the fires, scientists recorded from 50,000 to 1,000,000 lodgepole pine seeds per acre, or about one seed per square foot (10 seeds/m^2). The forest floor blossomed with colorful and luxuriant growths of fireweed, heartleaf arnica, wild strawberry and dandelion, leafy aster, and elk sedge within weeks of the blaze.

Relatively few mammals, especially bears and ungulates, died in the 1988 fires, and birds were able to escape the smoke and flames. The greatest mortality was probably among rodents. Some animal populations actually increased following the fires as altered plant succession and increased nutrient forage enhanced the availability of prey species, such as the populations of cavity-dwelling birds like mountain bluebirds, Barrow's goldeneyes, three-toed woodpeckers, house wrens, kestrels, and tree swallows. There were temporary displacements

of species, which depended on the late stages of plant succession, such as the pine marten. But there were increases in populations of ground dwellers and foragers, such as the blue grouse, as well as general increases in predator populations, including raptors, bears, and coyotes.

Because of the impact of the 1988 fires and the result of ecological assessment done by scientists since, the park's administration once again began, in 1992, a wildland fire management program that would allow naturally occurring fires to burn. Fire would continue to play its invigorating ecological role in the Greater Yellowstone Ecosystem while at the same time be controlled to avoid any duplications of the summer of 1988.

Left: An Elk seems lost in a burnt forest. The regrowth after fires usually delivers a bounty of new vegetation for the large ungulates. Wildlife losses during a wildfire are highest with populations of rodents and insects. Large animals are usually able to flee to safer ground.
Photo by Michael Quinton

Below: Charred trees on Mt. Washburn.
Photo by Charles Gurche

Ecology

story. Vegetation on the forest floor includes grouse whortleberry, elk sedge, heartleaf arnica, mosses, and lichens. Here and there, meadows and wet grasslands are interspersed among the lodgepole pines.

If fire is eliminated or suppressed in a sub-climax lodgepole pine forest, typical of much of the Greater Yellowstone region, shade-tolerant, understory spruce and fir will eventually penetrate the canopy and replace the lodgepole pine as the climax community.

In moist habitats and at higher elevations, Engelmann spruce and subalpine fir trees commonly dominate old forests. Where spruce and fir cannot grow, lodgepole pine or aspen are the most abundant trees.

Plant habitat types are controlled by factors such as temperature, precipitation, soil type, soil moisture, and exposure to the sun. Those conditions are largely determined by elevation. The average elevation in Yellowstone is about 8,000 feet (2,400m). As elevation (and latitude) increases, temperature decreases and precipitation increases, increasing soil moisture.

The plant and animal communities that will evolve in an area can be predicted by studying the local geologic composition. As rocks weather they contribute their mineral content to the local soil. Some rocks, such as the igneous rhyolites and tuffs ejected from the Yellowstone Caldera, are composed largely of quartz and potassium feldspar. Soils in those areas are nutrient-poor, do not hold water well, but support extensive, even-aged stands of drought-tolerant, shallow-rooted lodgepole pines. In contrast, andesite, an igneous rock common in the Absaroka Range, is composed mainly of iron, calcium, and magnesium minerals. When andesite rocks weather, they form nutrient-rich, water retaining soils which support more diverse plant communities such as mixed forests interspersed with moist meadows.

Lake sediments such as those underlying Hayden Valley, which were deposited during glacial periods, form clay soils that allow meadow communities to outcompete trees for water. The patches of lodgepole pines in Hayden Valley grow in areas of rhyolite rock outcrops.

Because the type of rocks, and the soils formed by their weathering, influences the development of plant communities, it follows that geology has an indirect effect on the distribution and movement of certain animals, especially herbivores and omnivores. For example, whitebark pine nuts are an important food source for

Above left: Blue columbine and sticky geranium can be found in cool moist areas of the park. Wildflowers constitute an important element in the diets of many of Yellowstone's animals. Seeds, are important to birds, nectar and pollen to insects, wild strawberries to squirrels and chipmunks, and flowers are even a prime staple for the largest of Yellowstone's predators: the grizzly bear.
Photo by Jeff Foott

Above: An often seen flower in the Greater Yellowstone Ecosystem: The Indian Paintbrush
Photo by Pat O'Hara

Left: A mixed flower scene near Tower. Wildflowers grow in profusion in Yellowstone especially during the period of Mid-June to Mid-August. They are everywhere and species presence will depend mostly on elevation, moisture, and quality of soil. They are found on the edges of geysers all the way to the highest and driest slopes.
Photo by Willard Clay

forty four

grizzly bears in the spring. The bears seek out middens of nuts cached by red squirrels and Clark's nutcrackers in the andesitic soils on Mt. Washburn, as these soils are favorable for the growth of the whitebark pine. Elk and bison frequent grasslands that thrive in the rich sedimentary soils of the Lamar and Hayden valleys. Even geyser basins, where vegetation is kept free from snow, are winter havens for wild ungulates.

The topography (a result of elevation) also affects vegetation through exposure. South-facing slopes tend to have more insolation, or exposure to sunlight, be warmer, and drier. North-facing slopes are more shaded, cooler, and moist.

Scientists have identified more than 40 known habitat types in Yellowstone, of which about 80% are forested. Of the various cover types in the park, only 15 are forested, and these are largely dominated by five coniferous species. Large areas of a specific habitat may be composed of several different covers and a given cover may extend over several habitats. Plant ecologists have further divided the park into five areas, or provinces, each with characteristic types of bedrock, soils, topography, and combinations of habitat types.

The Gallatin Range Province is forested with spruce-fir, and whitebark pine at higher elevations, and Douglas-fir at lower levels. Common understory plants include western meadowrue, fireweed, heartleaf arnica, grouse whortleberry, showy aster, sticky geranium, yampa, goldenrod, pinegrass, woods strawberry, and shiny-leaf spirea.

The Absaroka Range Province is forested with spruce, fir, and lodgepole pine, with whitebark pine common above 8,600 feet (2,620 m). Non-forest cover types include globe, huckleberry, Utah honeysuckle, Engelmann aster, Ross's sedge, pinegrass, elk sedge, cascade mountain-ash, and one-sided wintergreen.

The Central Plateaus Province is covered mostly by lodgepole pine, with scattered spruce and fir. The understory includes grouse whortleberry, elk sedge, heart-leaf arnica, mosses, and lichens. There are several areas of meadows and wet grassland.

The Southwest Plateaus Province is forested with lodgepole pine, subalpine fir, and Engelmann spruce. Common plants on the forest floor include elk sedge, one-side wintergreen, Ross's sedge, mountain sweetroot, mountain snowberry, serviceberry, early blue violet, tufted hairgrass, and Idaho fescue.

The Yellowstone-Lamar River Valleys Province is covered mostly by non-forest vegetation including big sagebrush, Idaho fescue, sticky geranium, California brome, graceful cinquefoil, sulfur buckwheat, and timber oatgrass. Forested areas are mostly Douglas-fir.

Above: A willow is outlined in alpenglow. Alpenglow can often be seen in high mountain areas as the red light from the setting sun is reflected on snow and ice.
Photo by Art Wolfe

Above right: Aspen bark and leaves contrast colors in fall. As the chlorophyll rich tree leaves are emptied of their green pigment in the fall, the leaves' main pigment are made apparent, thus the colors of fall. In this case, the Aspen leaves assume a rich golden hue.
Photo by Pat O'Hara

Right: Fall colors signal the soon to arrive deep snows of winter. The natural bounties of a short growing season will be replaced by lean and challenging months. It is a stressful change for all species in Yellowstone, a change they have adapted to survive for millions of years.
Photo by Adam Jones

The Greater Yellowstone Ecosystem

A legal boundary defines Yellowstone National Park. It encloses a 2.2 million acre (890,000 ha) area on a map. Boundaries suggest that things are securely contained within them; they imply ownership, a concept that has no meaning in nature. Animals and plants do not honor human territorial imperatives, instead it is the natural processes that link them. The boundary lines that people draw are often determined by topographic features, such as the crest of a mountain range or the path a river follows, and frequently by political borders. Wild organisms move freely across these arbitrary boundaries and lines on a map do not deter natural processes.

national parks (The Leopold Report) concluded, "... habitat is not a fixed or stable entity that can be set aside and preserved behind a fence, like a cliff dwelling or a petrified tree..." This concept is central to the idea of a greater ecosystem. An ecologist once coined the phrase "ghost acreage" to refer to areas beyond established boundaries of a natural system required to sustain and nurture the populations within those boundaries. Scientists and resource managers acknowledged these ecological truths and slowly, in the 60s, 70s and 80s, began to speak of a Greater Yellowstone Ecosystem (GYE), much larger than the park. The larger ecosystem concept, now widely

Above: Colter Peak, in the Absaroka Range, towers at 10,683 feet (3,256 m) above the Thorofare Country, the largest and most remote expanse of wilderness in the lower 48 States. This area is a haven for wildlife and represents the essence of the Greater Yellowstone Ecosystem. The GYE is an area recognized to be as large as 18 million acres or about 28,000 square miles (72,520 km²), about eight times the size of Yellowstone National Park and drawn not by legal boundaries but by the natural links that exists among all living species within. The infant Yellowstone River flows, from its source on the slopes of Yount Peak, through the spectacular valley of the Thorofare and empties into the southeast arm of Yellowstone Lake.
Photo by Tom Murphy

The grizzly bear's home range is larger than any land mammal, typically about 250 square miles (650 km²) for an adult male, and a mature grizzly can range over 1,000 square miles (2,590 km²) in a season. The migratory routes of elk, bison, and other ungulates carry them well beyond official park boundaries. The seasonal migration of the pronghorn is the longest migration of any land mammal in the lower 48 states taking them over 200 miles, from the Yellowstone and Grand Teton high country south to the Red Desert. Gray wolves are known to travel up to 60 miles (96 km) in a single night, and large wolf packs may cover a territory as large as 260 square miles (673 km²). Large wildfires burn freely and capriciously across legal boundaries. Forests and other plant communities do not stop at borders.

Four decades ago, a landmark report on the state of research in the

accepted, recognizes that Yellowstone is not an island isolated, and insulated, by drawn boundaries. Rather, the park is part of an ecological whole where surrounding lands and their health are vital for its survival.

Yellowstone National Park is just the 2.2 million acre core of a larger system that covers about 28,000 square miles (72,520 km²), or nearly 18 million acres (7.3 million ha). The GYE includes: Grand Teton National Park, a majestic park including the towering peaks of the Teton Range rising abruptly above the valley floor, as well as the John D. Rockefeller Jr. Memorial Parkway, an 82-mile corridor linking Yellowstone to Grand Teton National Park. In addition, the Gallatin National Forest borders the park on the north and northwest with more than 40% of its acreage designated as roadless wilderness. It includes the Absaroka-Beartooth, Gallatin and Madison mountain ranges. The Custer National Forest surrounds the northeast corner of the park, including the Beartooth Highway, labeled "the most scenic road in America," and part of the Beartooth plateau. The Shoshone National Forest, the nation's first national forest, flanks the eastern part of Yellowstone with 2.4 million acres (971,000 ha) of rugged terrain. It includes the North Absaroka Wilderness, and portions of the Beartooth Plateau, Absaroka, Beartooth, and the Wind River Ranges. The Bridger-Teton National Forest wraps around the southern edge of the park, including the isolated Thorofare area and includes 1.2 million acres (485,000 ha) of wilderness in the Teton, Gros Ventre and Bridger Wilderness. The Caribou-Targhee National Forest touches the southwestern and western boundaries of both Grand Teton and Yellowstone. The Beaverhead-Deerlodge National Forest just northwest of Yellowstone is part of the GYE too. The GYE also includes two National Wildlife Refuges, the National Elk Refuge and the Red Rock Lakes National Wildlife Refuge, as well as lands managed by the Bureau of Land Management. Altogether, federal lands total 13,900,000 acres (5.6 million ha). In addition, there are 500,000 acres (202,000 ha) of state land in Wyoming, Montana and Idaho, including land on three Indian reservations, and about 3.3 million acres (1.3 million ha) of private land within the ecosystem.

With the exception of the Alaskan wilderness, the greater

Above: The grizzly bear is more than a symbol of wildness in Yellowstone National Park. Because the grizzly's home range can cover an area as large as a 1,000 square miles (2,590 km²), the presence, health, and population growth of this species is indicative of the health of the environment in the Greater Yellowstone Ecosystem at large.
Photo by Tom Vezo / Minden Pictures

Below: The area of the park surrounding Pelican Creek marks the center of the Grizzly range in the Greater Yellowstone Ecosystem. This area of the park, east of Fishing Bridge, is prime habitat for the "great bear" and many other species. This creek was named after one of the great bird was mistaken for a goose and-shot by a prospector.
Photo by Henry H. Holdsworth

Yellowstone area may be the largest, biologically richest and most complex ecosystem in North America. Greater numbers and varieties of animal species live in Yellowstone than any other place in the coterminous United States. The GYE is also one of the few remaining large, relatively unaltered, and self-regulating temperate zone ecosystems on the planet and has not yet suffered the rapid acceleration of natural change that results from extensive human manipulation. It has remained an essentially pristine vignette of primitive North America.

Still, there are persistent threats to its integrity as a wild system, in spite of its relative remoteness. Habitat loss and fragmentation, human population growth, deterioration of air and water quality, proliferation of non-native species, increasing physical developments, and differing policies of resource management agencies within the system are among the problems. Habitat fragmentation is a particularly insidious threat to species approaching the one-way-road to extinction. It is like randomly removing pieces from a completed jigsaw puzzle across which those animals must move to survive.

To help promote the concept of a greater ecosystem and to defend its heath, survival and management, organizations such as the Greater Yellowstone Coalition (GYC) and the Greater Yellowstone Coordinating Committee (GYCC) were formed by private voluntary interests, as well as by coordinated management of local, state, and federal organizations. These organizations are working today to ensure that managing the resources is not done in a fragmented manner, but instead in a coordinated fashion considering the entire ecosystem.

However, in managing this large ecosystem, management concerns must also be applied to areas beyond, or geographically isolated from the boundaries of the GYE. The preservation of corridors for wildlife movement among disarticulated habitats being of prime concern. The Yellowstone to Yukon Conservation Initiative (or Y2Y) was created to do just that. A joint Canadian-U.S. network of over 340 organizations, institutions and foundations, with the help of many more conservation-minded individuals, is working to restore and maintain the unique natural heritage of the Yellowstone to Yukon region. Having as its principal objective that "... the Yellowstone to Yukon region continues to function as an interconnected web of life, capable of supporting all of the natural and human communities that reside within it, for now and for future generations."

Above left: The 25,000-acre National Elk Refuge is located in Jackson Hole, south of Yellowstone. It serves mostly as a winter (November-May) home for more than 7,000 elk, where they are fed during the most difficult days of winter. During the summer and early fall the elk population spreads throughout their local range, which includes a large part of Yellowstone National Park.
Photo by Raymond K. Gehman

Above right: The Beartooth Mountains along the picturesque Beartooth Highway is the largest Alpine Tundra area in the lower 48 states. This area of the Absaroka-Beartooth Wilderness serves as a spectacular approach to the Northeast Entrance of Yellowstone National Park.
Photo by Raymond K. Gehman

Left: The dramatic Teton Range and the Snake River. Grand Teton National Park protects more than 310,000 acres or about 500 square miles (125,000 ha, 1,294 km^2), and constitutes with Yellowstone, just to the north, the heart of the Greater Yellowstone Ecosystem.
Photo by Londie G. Padelsky

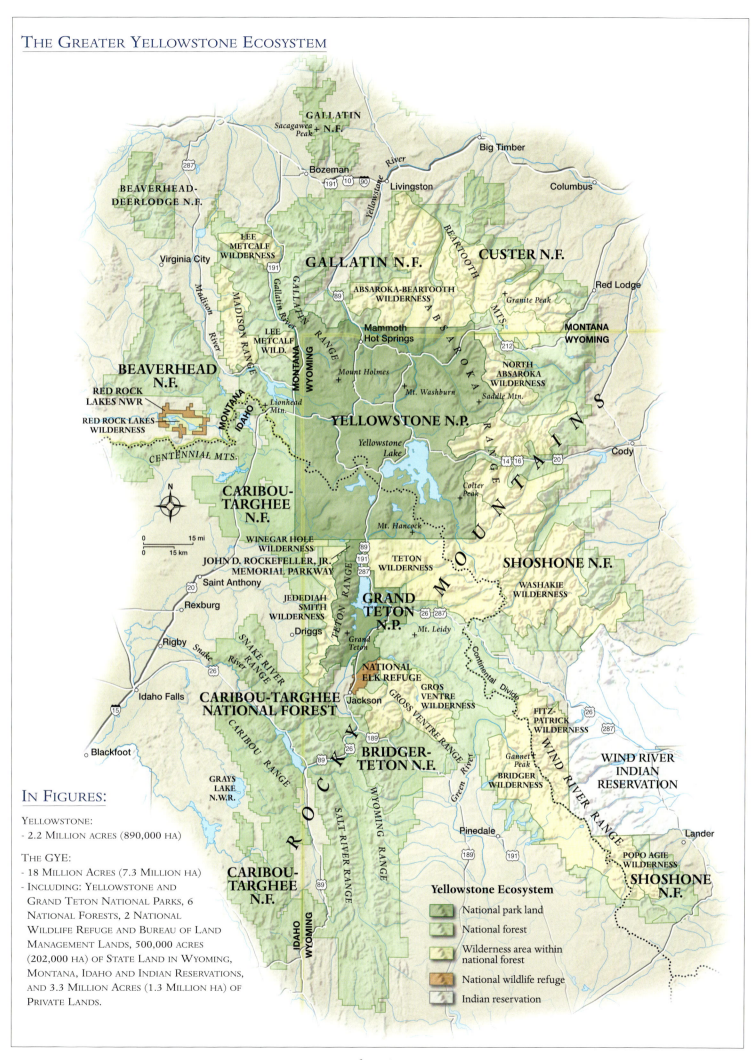

WILDLIFE

Wild animals were commonplace to the mountain men and explorers of the 19th Century. The spectacular geothermal eruptions in the Yellowstone region, which few people had seen before, impressed them more than the abundant wildlife. Preservation of the geysers, hot springs, and other features was the main impetus for the establishment of Yellowstone National Park. Still, as advancing civilization took its toll on the historic fauna of the west, Yellowstone's value as a refuge for diminishing animal populations assumed greater national significance.

The violent volcanic episodes, which created the Yellowstone calderas and the central plateau, and later periods of glaciation, probably killed or displaced most animals in the region. Still, some living things survived and, since the end of the Great Ice Age 10,000 years ago, a great variety of animals has flourished.

In Yellowstone, there are no walls, moats or fences, no artificial habitats or carefully concealed barricades. Animals are truly wild here; free to wander without restraint, through an environment that has largely remained unchanged for centuries. One of the largest and most unique wildlife populations on the continent lives and interacts in this remnant of primitive North America. Animals, large and small, occupy every habitat. A tiny ephydrid fly, darting about in the sulfurous mist above a geyser runoff channel, is as significant as a grizzly bear. Every species fills a special ecological niche. All are eating or being eaten. All are connected through the wonderful intricacies of natural processes such as food chains by which energy

The imprint of a swift end! A small rodent fell prey to a hunting hawk, another chapter in the fight for survival in one of the last wild place in the lower 48 states. There have been 319 species of birds identified in Yellowstone, 148 of which are known to nest in the park. The avian fauna includes 18 birds-of-prey such as the bald eagle, the osprey, and the peregrine falcon.
Photo by Tom Murphy

is transferred through the system. All are adapted to extremes of weather and climate.

The animals of the Yellowstone region are more diverse than in most other areas of the continent. There are few other places in North America where one can begin to experience the richness of the fauna of pre-Columbian North America. And yet, it is not the relative richness that is important; rather, it is the surprising integrity of the living community that is most significant. It is virtually unaltered (except along the narrow corridors of human access and use) from the time of the Native American and mountain man. This near completeness of the flora and fauna is all the more striking in a natural world grown increasingly smaller in relation to its fabricated counterpart. With the recent restoration of the gray wolf, the area is believed to have a nearly complete native vertebrate population, with all of its ecological associations intact. The only member of the historic fauna that remains missing from the park is the black-footed ferret.

The black-footed ferret suffered the same fate that befell the gray wolf. Campaigns to poison or shoot ferrets as pests, disease, and increased agriculture caused black-footed ferret populations to shrink. In 1967, the black-footed ferret had been eliminated from 98 percent of its historic range, including low-elevation plains and sagebrush steppe environments in the Greater Yellowstone Ecosystem (GYE). Still, a small surviving population was discovered in 1981 near Meeteetse, Wyoming, just 30 miles or so from the eastern margin of the Greater Yellowstone region. As a result of captive breeding and conservation

Left: An elk bugles at sunset. The haunting and powerful shriek of the bull elk is heard in the fall during the rut. The elk is the second largest deer in North America after the moose. A large male can weigh up to 1,100 lbs (495 kg) and carry a set of antlers as long as 50 inches (1,20 m). The elk population in the GYE, estimated at more than 90,000 animals, is the largest in North America.
Photo by Henry H. Holdsworth

Right: Bison warming themselves in the Upper Geyser Basin in the winter. The geothermal energy of Yellowstone forms microenvironments where bison and other ungulates find warmth and accessible vegetation during the coldest periods of the year, thus helping their survival.
Photo by Jeff Henry

Wildlife

efforts, breeding populations of the black-footed ferret are gradually being returned to the wild in the Northern Rocky Mountains, but not yet in the park.

In the GYE there are 311 species of birds, from tiny finches to the endangered peregrine falcon and trumpeter swan. In its lakes and streams there are 18 species of fish; 12 of which are native to the area. A dozen reptiles and amphibians are found here, among them the prairie rattlesnake, the western chorus frog, and the Rocky Mountain rubber boa. The 60 known species of mammals include all of the large North American ungulates, as well as others, ranging from the tiny and voracious masked shrew to the legendary grizzly, or "Great Bear."

In nature, there always are larger numbers of small organisms than large ones. Twelve thousand species of insects have been identified in the area ranging from butterflies to beetles; ants to mosquitoes; and wasps to salmonflies. In addition, there are millions of individual invertebrates, such as diatoms and rotifers, which go largely unnoted, but are critical to nutrient recycling and energy flow through the system. A pyramid of numbers, with a grizzly bear at its top, is built from millions of pine nuts, truffles, berries, army cutworm moths, ants; thousands of pocket gophers and voles; hundreds of lake trout; and, tens of bison and elk calves.

Yellowstone's mammal fauna includes one of the two remaining sizable, self-regulating grizzly bear populations in the lower 48 states. While its population has increased in recent years (it was estimated in 1996 that their number was between 280 and 610 individuals with at least 70 cubs), the grizzly may be the species most vulnerable to the fragmentation of the ecosystem. The grizzly's smaller relative, the black bear, is present in larger numbers, but neither species is as frequently seen as in the past. This is, however, not an indication of decreasing numbers. In recent years, more enlightened wildlife management policies have eliminated artificial feeding, a practice that led to the frequent appearance of bears at roadsides and garbage dumps.

In fact, for many years, the National Park Service actually encouraged artificial feeding by conducting interpretive lectures at garbage dumps, where curious visitors were seated in bleachers to observe the spectacle. Visitors also freely fed bears marshmallows, cookies and all sorts of human fare from their cars, a practice, which often led to lengthy "bear jams" and dangerous encounters

Above left: A coyote hunts in the snow. With a very acute sense of hearing and smell, the coyote searches and listens for any sign of prey. Once located, the prey is pounced upon for a quick meal.
Photo by Ron Niebrugge

Above: A red fox pup is on the alert. Foxes are the smallest wild canids in Yellowstone.
Photo by Jeff Henry

Left: A frost-covered coyote howls. A very adaptive member of the dog family (Canidae) the coyote is present in nearly every habitat of the park and can be observed at any time of the day. They stand at about 2 feet (60 cm) at the shoulders and are much smaller than a wolf. They were hunted mercilessly in the park between 1907 and 1925 when more than 3,000 were killed. They are an integral part of the GYE, playing an important role in the control of rodent populations.
Photo by Jeff Henry

with many "habituated" bears along park roads and near campsites.

These misguided activities were abated several decades ago, as resource managers learned more about bear behavior. Deprived of unhealthy food sources, bears have simply dispersed back into more remote sections of the park, a much healthier situation for bears and people. There are about 500 to 600 black bears in the park, which are more frequently seen than the Grizzly.

Predators range in size from a grizzly bear that may weigh 700 pounds (320 kg), the largest ever recorded weighing almost 1,500 lbs (680 kg), to a hoary bat that weighs only a fraction of an ounce, (a few grams) or a black-winged damselfly feeding on mosquitoes.

Other predators include, coyotes, red foxes, bobcats, river otters, pine martens, badgers, long-tailed weasels, great gray owls, ospreys, harlequin ducks, bald eagles, about 20 mountain lions, and the rare wolverine. Gray wolves, past victims of persecution and misguided management, and long absent from the GYE, have been successfully restored. They now number 306 individuals in about 31 packs with 174 in 14 packs residing within the park.

Sadly, there are more than 40 species of vertebrates and hundreds of invertebrates, within the park, which are listed as rare, threatened or even endangered. Only time will tell if they survive because, as development increases in the region, the possibility of habitat fragmentation and loss is ever-present. This threat motivates scientists and resource managers to be vigilant, to continue their study of the connections among animal populations, and to adopt multiple species management in the context of a larger ecosystem.

Elk, also known by the Shawnee Indian word "wapiti," are the most easily and frequently seen large mammals in the park. The Yellowstone elk population level varies with the severity of winter, predation by wolves, and range conditions, but is close to 15,000-20,000 individuals, in several migratory herds of varying size. Combined with other herds in the region, there may be about 90,000 elk throughout the GYE, making it the largest herd in North America.

The largest wild, free-ranging population of American bison remaining on the continent, about 4,000 animals, is composed of three herds, located in the Lamar, Pelican, Hayden and Firehole valleys. The North American bison population, thought to have been almost 60 million in the 1800s, was reduced to fewer than 50 animals by the beginning of the 20th century. The bison was saved from extinction at a ranch in the Lamar Valley of Yellowstone National Park, where its numbers gradually increased. The American bison, the largest terrestrial animal in North America, is commonly but incorrectly called the buffalo, a name more properly applied to the cape buffalo of Africa. Bison are frequently seen throughout the park.

Above right: A black bear naps in the shade. There are approximately 500 to 600 black bears in Yellowstone. A mature male may weigh up to 600 lbs (270 kg) with females reaching 350 lbs (160 kg). Omnivorous and busy eaters, they can be seen at any time of the day.
Photo by Jeff Henry

Above: A female grizzly protects a bison carcass as her three cubs look on. The grizzly bear is a large animal; adult males averaging 400 to 600 lbs (181 and 270 kg) but sometimes reaching over 1,000 lbs (450 kg) and females about 550 lbs (250 kg). It is about 4 ½ feet (1.3 m) at the shoulder hump and reaches 8 feet (2.4 m) on its hind legs.
Photo by Tom Murphy

Right: A grizzly bear is in pursuit of a bison calf as the bison mother tries to defend her young. Omnivorous and powerful, the grizzly does not shy-away from hunting large mammals such as elk and bison.
Photo by Joel Sartore

Wildlife

Shira's moose, of which there are less than 1,000 in the park, are often encountered in open meadows and along stream courses. They are large, clumsy-looking animals, but surprisingly swift and graceful. Moose may be seen in Willow Park south of Mammoth, in meadows near Canyon Village and Lake, and in the Snake River area to the south. Moose are the largest members of the deer family in the world, and have massive antlers that look a little like palm fronds.

The mule deer population is close to 2,300. Mule deer, also commonly called the black-tailed deer, summer at higher elevations, but move down to warmer, sheltered valleys during the long winters. Unlike white-tailed deer, relatives with a characteristic large "flag" tail seen occasionally in lower elevation grass and shrub lands, mule deer have short, black tails, and very large ears. Deer tend to move down to drink at streams and rivers at dusk. Large herds of deer may often be seen in nearby open fields.

Rocky Mountain bighorn sheep are sure-footed rock climbers and jumpers. There are up to 225 bighorns in the park. They may be seen negotiating the steep walls of the Gardiner River Canyon near Mammoth Hot Springs, or along the North fork of the Shoshone River during the winter. In the summer, Bighorns move to higher elevations, such as the slopes of Mount Washburn. They are distinguished by massive curled horns, especially in males.

Male bighorns, competing for females during the fall rutting period, charge each other, crashing their heads together at speeds of more than 20 miles an hour (32 km/h). These head-butting battles can continue for hours, and make sounds that can be heard a mile or more away. A band of Shoshone Indians, called the Sheepeaters, depended largely on mountain sheep for their livelihood.

Pronghorns are found in lower, drier, sagebrush-steppe and plains environments. They can sometimes be seen near the north entrance to the park, in the Lamar Valley, and near the North Fork of the Shoshone River. Pronghorns look like they were imported from the Serengeti Plain of East Africa. Despite its generic name *Antilocapra*, meaning "antelope goat," the pronghorn is neither an antelope nor a goat, nor is it even closely related. It is the sole remnant of an ancient ungulate family dating back 20 million years. They are distinctively and unmistakably colored, with a reddish coat and white markings. Pronghorns, which number about 250 in the park, are capable of running at speeds of 70 miles an hour (112 km/h). They can leap nearly 30 feet in a single bound; yet they cannot jump fences like deer.

Above left: An elk in velvet. The antlers of all deer, including the large moose, are shed every year. As they regrow in spring, they are covered with a velvety layer of vascularized skin that nourishes the growing bone. When at full size, the skin dies and is scraped off against bushes and trees.
Photo by Jeff Henry

Above: A mule deer fawn wears his camouflaged white spotted coat. They are commonly born as twins, usually in June or early July, after a gestation of 7 months.
Photo by Tom Murphy

Left: A bugling elk in rut looks over his harem of cows. The male elk is challenged many times during the rut, between late August and early November, by other bulls. Violent head butting clashes often occur to establish dominance. After reproduction and a gestation of 8½ months, a calf is born, usually during the first part of June.
Photo by James Randklev

A seventh large ungulate was introduced to the region several years ago to provide game for hunters. The shaggy, white-coated mountain goat is a creature of high elevations. They are sure-footed mountain climbers thanks to elastic pads on the bottom of their hooves. Although successful in this environment, it is not a part of the original fauna of the Greater Yellowstone area as it is in Glacier National Park farther to the north. Mountain goats are sometimes seen on the Beartooth Plateau. The mountain goat is not a true goat, but is related to the chamois species of Europe and Asia.

A common characteristic of wild ungulates is either horns or antlers. True horns are simple unbranched structures that are never shed. They are always found in male bison, bighorn sheep, mountain goats, and pronghorns, and not always in females. They consist of an outgrowth of the skull's frontal bone, covered by a layer of keratin, the same substance that forms human fingernails. Horns grow throughout the life of the animal. Males use horns as weapons when competing for females, and both sexes use their horns as defensive shields to ward off predators. The pronghorn is the only one to shed only part of its horns, the outer sheath, each year.

The antlers of male deer, elk, and moose are not horns. Antlers are bony outgrowths of the frontal bone, but they are shed each year after the mating season. They begin to grow in early summer and are covered with a velvety layer of skin with short, fine hairs. The velvet contains a network of blood vessels that nourishes the growing bone. Antlers reach full size by late summer, and the layer of velvet dries up, shrinks, and falls off.

In some countries, elk antlers sold in a powdered form, are thought to have medicinal properties, and are highly valued. This has unfortunately led to substantial and highly profitable illegal harvesting of shed antlers throughout the Yellowstone region.

Biologists estimate that there are 20 to 35 cougars, or mountain lions, in the park, 300 beaver, and variable numbers of foxes, badgers, river otters, weasels, martens, lynx and other small mammals. Rare wolverines have also been observed.

People tend to be preoccupied by the large and spectacular mammals, but there are more than 50 smaller mammals, some seldom seen, that play important roles in the natural processes of the larger ecosystem. In numbers they far exceed their showier, more charismatic, relatives. Many of them are so small and secretive that they are seldom seen. Sometimes their trails, burrows, or nests are the only evidence of their presence. Still, they are key to the survival of the larger critters. A coyote may feed on red-backed voles, northern pocket gophers, snowshoe hares, Uintah ground squirrels, deer mice, desert cottontails, pygmy shrews, frogs, toads, and occasional

Above: A mule deer buck, unmistakable with large ears and double branched antler tines. Their population in the park migrates according to the seasons; spending the summer at higher elevations and the winter near warmer valley bottoms.
Photo by Henry H. Holdsworth

Above right: The bighorn sheep enjoys the higher elevations of the park with rocky slopes.
Photo by Marc Muench

Right: A male Shira's moose stands in a bog. This species is smaller than the largest of all deer, the Alaskan moose, but males can reach weights of 1,400 lbs (630 kg) and a shoulder height of 7 ½ feet (2.25 m). There are probably less than 1,000 moose in Yellowstone. They are usually found near bogs, sloughs, beaver ponds, and willow areas.
Photo by Shin Yoshino/Minden

A Homecoming

Wolves once ranged widely throughout North America, from the Arctic tundra to Mexico. As people began to occupy and develop more of the landscape, especially during the westward expansion of the country, wolf habitat was drastically diminished. Wolves were labeled

as dangerous predators, as "bad" animals, and deliberate extermination programs were undertaken. Although he became an outspoken advocate for the restoration of wild predator species, Theodore Roosevelt once referred to wolves as "the beasts of waste and desolation."

The gray wolf was part of the historic native fauna of the Yellowstone country, but intensive control efforts eliminated it from the area by the 1940s. Wolves were the only missing carnivore in the otherwise largely intact historic fauna in the Greater Yellowstone Ecosystem until a few years ago.

During the past few decades, research has clarified the role that the wolf plays in maintaining balance in a naturally functioning ecosystem. Scientists know that predator-prey relationships, such as the one that links wolves to elk, are essential parts of food chains that transfer energy from one species to another. Researchers also know that wolf predation helps to keep elk populations at optimum levels by eliminating old, sick and injured elk from the herds.

The Greater Yellowstone Ecosystem was large enough to accommodate a wolf-pack home range and it had an abundant population of prey animals. After decades of debate on whether or not to restore the gray wolf to the Yellowstone Ecosystem, 31 gray wolves from Canada were released in Yellowstone in 1995 and early 1996. Wolves had come home. They were the first to roam Yellowstone since the 1930s. The goal was to maintain at least 10 breeding wolf pairs in the Greater Yellowstone Ecosystem and in each of the two other recovery areas in central Idaho and northwestern Montana.

Yellowstone's restored wolf population has thrived, with relatively few conflicts with human activities adjacent to the park. As of March 2004, about 306 wolves roamed the Greater Yellowstone Area, including dozens of pups born the previous spring. The wolves were traveling in at least 31 packs, with several solitary wolves wandering alone, seeking mates, or in groups that did not have a breeding pair. U.S. Fish and Wildlife Service criteria for delisting wolves as endangered or threatened in the combined recovery areas, of Montana, Idaho, and Wyoming, call for at least 30 breeding pairs, equally and uniformly distributed, for three successive years. The end of 2003 met those recovery goals and it is likely that the wolf population in the Rocky Mountain area will be considered viable and fully recovered.

Each wolf restored to Yellowstone is assigned a number. The last of the original 14 wolves restored to Yellowstone in 1995, wolf #2, died in 2003. Other wolves killed her after she lost her dominant role. She had mated with wolf #7 and they established the first new pack in the park in 1996. That pack was called the Leopold Pack, named in honor of conservationist Aldo Leopold who had advocated restoration in 1944. The Leopold Pack always numbered about 12 wolves and it never left the park. Wolf #2 had produced 8 litters and at least 29 of her pups survived beyond the first year.

In February 2004, another of the original Canadian wolves restored to Yellowstone, was killed in a territorial dispute with wolves from another pack. The 8-year-old dominant, or alpha female of the Druid Peak Pack, wolf #42

was the only one of the original 28 wolves that remained in the park. Her sister, wolf #41, is now the only survivor of the original group, but she lives outside of the park in the Sunlight Basin near Cody, Wyoming.

Author and conservationist Romain Gary was speaking about an aging elephant when he wrote *A Love Letter to an Old Companion*, but his words are a tribute to all wild creatures, including the wolves that have come home to Yellowstone. He said, "…your presence among us carries a resonance that cannot be accounted for in terms of science or reason, but only in terms of awe, wonder and reverence."

Above left: Members of the Rose Creek Pack in the Lamar Valley. A carnivore, feeding mostly on larger prey such as deer, moose, and elk, the gray wolf also preys on smaller animals such as rodents. It usually hunts in organized packs to down larger animals.
Photo by Joel Sartore

Above: The largest member of the Canid family the gray wolf (canis lupus) is a powerful animal reaching 125 pounds for a male and about 70 for a female (56 and 31 kg). Social, they live in packs where the alpha male and female exercise leadership over other pack members. The alpha female is usually the only female to reproduce. With a gestation period just over 2 months, a litter of up to 7 pups is born in protective areas and dens.
Photo by Jeff Henry

Left: As wolves were restored to Yellowstone the elk knew right away what to do when faced with this ancestral foe. They searched for safety in numbers, and spent less time in valleys and river bottoms where they had little protective cover.
Photo by Joel Sartore

birds. Whitebark pine nuts, harvested by red squirrels and Clark's nutcrackers and cached in middens throughout the forest, are later visited by grizzly bears emerging from their winter sleep.

Birds represent the greatest species diversity among vertebrates in Yellowstone. About 319 species, including 148 species that are known to nest in the region, have been recorded in the park. These include species passing through, on their way to different locations. Most birds found in Yellowstone migrate to lower elevations and more southern latitudes starting in September.

Biologists are carefully monitoring the status of several bird species. The threatened bald eagle population appears to be recovering, with 32 nests and 24 fledgling eaglets noted in 2003. Captive-bred (and formerly endangered) peregrine falcons were released in Yellowstone during the 1980s, but restoration was stopped in

Above left: Predators come in all sizes. This short-tailed weasel will continue to hunt during the coldest months of the year, looking for rodents and other small prey. A relative of the the mink, otter, badger, wolverine, and marten, the diminutive weasel is a voracious predator.
Photo by Henry H. Holdsworth

Above right: A coyote feeding on the carcass of a bison, probably a victim of old age or the cold winter. Yellowstone is a true living ecosystem, with predators and prey, ever dancing a ballet of life, survival, and death. The proximity of roads and tourist attractions does not diminish the wildness of this park. With the help of sound management policies, Yellowstone can remain a natural haven for all; "The first of the last wild places."
Photo by Jeff Vanuga

Below: Bison roaming in the snow. The winter represents a hard challenge for all species of Yellowstone. Deep snowpack, cold temperatures, and roaming predators are all obstacles to survival.
Photo by Thomas Mangelsen / Minden Pictures

Wildlife

1988 because the peregrine population was increasing naturally. During 2003, 23 nests produced 49 young falcons. The osprey population has varied, but a recent low of 38 pairs and 17 young birds was recorded. Biologists are also keeping a close eye on American white pelicans, common loons, harlequin ducks, great gray owls, and various colonial nesting birds. Researchers believe that the population of the trumpeter swan, the largest waterfowl in North America, is recovering from earlier lows. In 2003, there were 300 to 350 swans residing in the GYE, including 16 in the park.

A great variety of perching birds, warblers, wrens, finches, sparrows, blackbirds, tanagers, buntings, and others, add sound and color to the air. Various ducks, geese, grebes, herons, egrets and other water-loving birds, such as the American dipper and belted kingfisher, are attracted to the many lakes, streams and rivers of Yellowstone. The dipper, once known

Above left: A pronghorn buck. The American pronghorn is the fastest land mammal of the continent, capable of reaching speeds of 70 mph (112 km/h).
Photo by Jeff Vanuga

Above right: A pika rests on a rock. These small rodents are known for building miniature "hay stacks," or reserves of grasses and weeds, which they use for feed during the winter.
Photo by Tom Murphy

Below: A herd of bison in Hayden Valley near the Yellowstone River with views of the Washburn Mountains in the background. The Yellowstone bison population numbers approximately 4,000 animals. Nomadic grazers of grasses and sedges they wander from the high plateaus in summer to lower elevation meadows and open forest areas during winter. Powerful shoulder muscles allow bison to move their heads from side-to-side against deep snow to reach their food.
Photo by Jeff Henry

as the water ouzel, is always found near rapids and fast-moving water. In deeper areas, it dives into the water and runs along the bottom with half-open wings, searching for aquatic insects.

There really are only two seasons in the park, a short, mild summer, and a long winter with short days, bitter temperatures, and deep snow. Winter is a very stressful survival challenge for wild animals, and most of them are physically, physiologically, or behaviorally adapted to the severe conditions.

Hibernation is perhaps the best-known winter adaptation. It is a state of inactivity, or regulated hypothermia, in an animal brought about by short day lengths, cold temperatures and limited food sources. With huge drops in heart rate, body temperature and metabolism, a state of long term dormancy begins. During hibernation, the body temperature is only a few degrees above freezing, oxygen consumption is down to 2% of normal, and the heart rate drops from up to 300 beats a minute to just three or four. For the ground squirrel, for example, the respiratory rate drops from a normal of 200 per minute to 4 to 5, and the heart rate from 150 to 5.

True hibernators, such as Uintah and golden-mantled ground squirrels, yellow-bellied marmots, least chipmunks, bats and other mammals prepare for hibernation by building up large amounts of body fat. Some biologists refer to hibernation as "time migration," because it allows the animal to skip over the cold, stressful seasons and only expend itself fully in those months of abundant food and moderate climatic conditions.

Bears are not true hibernators. Instead, as winter weather begins, they search for a secure den, or "hibernaculum" and enter a less profound inactive state called "winter sleep" or "torpor." They too feed heavily during the fall, bulking up with fat reserves, and they may sleep for several months. Their

heart rate may drop from 40 to 10 beats per minutes, but their body temperature, normally about 100°F (37.7°C), only drops a few degrees, and seldom drops lower than 88°F (31.1°C). If bears are disturbed or stimulated during winter they may awaken, and sometimes leave their dens for short periods. Females give birth to cubs and nurse them during the winter.

Some true hibernators, including the yellow-bellied marmots, and others, enter protected burrows or dens, sometimes underground, and build nests of grass and other vegetation. In the winter den, the hibernators reduce surface-to-volume ratio to conserve heat by curling up in a ball with their extremities tucked tightly against the body. When the animals' body temperature coincides with the external temperature its respiration is imperceptible and it does not react to external stimuli. A true hibernator can even be handled without reacting. Circulatory system adaptations allow their brain to remain a few degrees warmer than the outside temperature, thus keeping its temperature constant even as the temperature of the skin changes. The nervous system is similarly adapted to maintain, reg-

Above: The badger, known for its fierce character, here protects his den among the remnants of a burned forest. Easily recognized by his white facial markings the badger is an excellent burrower and hunter of ground squirrels, gophers and other small rodents.
Photo by Michael S. Quinton/Minden

Above right: A group of Uintah ground squirrels are on the lookout. They are seen throughout Yellowstone, especially along the roads in the Lamar and Hayden valleys.
Photo by Shin Yoshino/Minden

Right: A calf bison plays with its mother. Bison breed in summer, usually from mid-July to mid-August. After a gestation of 9 months, a single calf, rarely two, is delivered in May or early June. Reddish-brown, the calves can easily be spotted among the herd. They are weaned the following spring.
Photo by Tom Murphy

Wildlife

Birds remaining in the area during cold weather, will benefit from the great insulation provided by their feathers. A half-inch-thick layer of feathers can keep birds up to 100°F (37°C) warmer than the ambient temperatures. Some birds fluff-up their back feathers, thus trapping more air and providing them with even more insulation.

There are many other fascinating behavioral and physiological adaptations to winter among the animals of Yellowstone. Pikas, red squirrels and beavers harvest and store food in accessible places before the arrival of cold weather and snow. These caches provide a ready source of food throughout the winter. Pikas harvest stems and leaves of various plants, and form them into miniature "haystacks" to dry among the rocks. Red squirrels harvest whitebark pine, spruce, and other conifer cones and cache them in mounds, or middens, on the forest floor, some as large as 15 by 30 feet (4 by 10 m).

ulate and coordinate essential metabolic processes. Weight loss is common during hibernation because of the lowered metabolism and as much as 40% of the total body weight may be lost.

Another common way that larger animals such as deer, elk, bison, and bighorn sheep minimize the rigors of winter is vertical migration. Wild ungulates move to lower, warmer valleys, or seek refuge in thermal areas where winter forage remains available. Deer, elk, and bison often follow one another through deep snow in long lines, a behavior that helps conserve energy. Bison and elk opportunistically follow trails and roads that have been groomed for over-snow vehicle travel.

Not all migrations are local. Gifted with the power of flight, many land birds and song birds, including swallows, sparrows, warblers, and blackbirds, known as neotropical migrants, are capable of escaping winter altogether by migrating to warmer places. These birds summer in the GYE and winter in the neotropics, many in western Mexico. Other species that make annual flights to the south include: American white pelicans, northern harriers and other hawks, peregrine falcons, American kestrels, redheads, canvasbacks, green-winged teals, mallards and other ducks, rufus hummingbirds, and American pipits.

Many small rodents, such as deer mice and jumping mice, huddle together in burrows to stay warm. The northern pocket gopher and other small mammals live under the snow where they are insulated and safe from predators. After the snowmelt, gopher "cores," long serpentine coils of earth left behind as gophers burrowed through the snow and filled the burrows with soil, remain. Northern flying squirrels keep warm in nests of shredded bark in abandoned woodpecker holes, in snags, or sometimes in nests anchored to branches. They feed on nuts and seeds that they have stored under the snow at the base of the trees.

The pelage of most mammal consists of a layer of longer guard hairs and short under fur. Longer,

Above left: With a wingspan reaching 8 feet (2.4 m) and a weight of 25-30 lbs (11-16 kg), the Trumpeter swan is the world's largest swan and the largest waterfowl in North America. Named for their trumpet-like call, they were once on the brink of extinction because of habitat destruction and plume hunting. Their population is making a small comeback. In 2003, a count showed 16 residing in the park with about 300 present in the GYE. Their winter numbers are augmented by migrating birds staying in Yellowstone. Magnificent birds they mate for life.
Photo by Michael S. Quinton/Minden

Above: A male yellow-headed blackbird. These birds are easily spotted, and heard, along marshes and ponds where they favor the cattails. They are active and curious.
Photo by Henry H. Holdsworth

Left: A nesting sandhill crane. They can often be seen in meadows hunting insects, rodents, and amphibians.
Photo by Henry H. Holdsworth

colorless, and hollow guard hairs contain trapped air that insulates and protects the under fur. Mammals molt, or shed, their lighter coats before winter arrives, and extra short, thick, often wavy under fur grows. Some have glands adjacent to each hair, secreting oil to waterproof the winter fur. Like birds and their feathers, mammals can fluff their fur to trap air when they are cold, and flatten it down to remove insulating air when they are warm. As spring arrives, large mammals molt and often appear to have thick patches of fur hanging from them. Some smaller mammals have their fur change color for winter, from dark to white. A form of camouflage for both prey and predators, like snowshoe hares and weasels. White hair also provides an additional layer of insulation as it contains more air and less pigment.

To be able to reach its food in often deep snow, the bison has developed large and powerful shoulder muscles attached to elongated vertebrae. Forming a distinctive hump, this adaptation allows the massive animal to move its head from side to side against the snow, effectively pushing it away from the food.

The moose, unlike elk and deer, does not push its way through snow but instead benefits from specially adapted leg joints which allow it to swing its legs in a circular motion over the snow.

Some of the smallest animals of the park have also developed some of the most fascinating adaptations to winter. In freezing or sub-freezing temperatures, as ice slowly forms inside its body, the chorus frog becomes severely diabetic. As a result the liver begins to convert glycogen to glucose which enters the blood stream and functions as an antifreeze. Within eight hours the frog's blood sugar rises 200-fold and effectively protects the internal organs against deep freeze as the frog's heart and breathing stop. As winter ends and warmer temperatures arrive, the heart resumes beating within an hour of thawing.

In all wildlife populations, there is a natural tendency toward a state of dynamic equilibrium with the physical environment and its plant communities. Throughout the year, the policy of the National Park Service is to preserve Yellowstone's wildlife resources in as nearly a pristine state as possible and no hunting or other wildlife harvesting is allowed. Wildlife and other resource managers working in Yellowstone, make science-based decisions intended to allow natural population regulation to occur through predation, harsh winters, changing range conditions, and other factors. Human intervention in natural processes is limited and consistent with visitor safety as,

Above left: Peregrine falcons were successfully restored to the Greater Yellowstone Area after a release program of captive-bred individuals was begun in 1980. Their population had been decimated by pesticides, especially DDT.
Photo by Jeff Vanuga

Above right: A great-gray owl surveying the snow surface for any signs of prey. The owl's incredible sense of hearing is coupled with near-silent flight to surprise small prey such as rodents.
Photo by Jim Fitzharris

Right: The bald eagle is a very large bird with a wingspan of more than 7 feet (2,10 m) and a height of about 30-45 inches (1 m). They are usually found along the lakes and rivers of Yellowstone, flying by, or perched in nearby trees, observing the water for signs of fish and waterfowl. There are approximately 24 nesting pairs of bald eagles in the park. Mature birds carry the distinctive white head and neck, yellow bill and near black body. Immature birds to five years are nearly completely brown.
Photo by Tom Murphy

Wildlife

for example, the euthanization or relocation of a bear that has repeatedly threatened campers, or consistent with the protection of native species against the spread of non-native and invasive species as for the protection of the park's waters against the New-Zealand mud snail, whirling disease, and lake trout. Habitat fragmentation by development of visitor use facilities is also minimized.

In Yellowstone, people are visitors in the house that nature built. Wildlife has a prior right to this place. The wildlife species in the park live in an environment very little changed since pre-Columbian time. They are able to live their lives and interact with others free from human intervention and, with the exception of developed areas, many animals live their entire lives without ever encountering a human being.

Still, the dark shadow of civilization approaches the park from all sides. In pursuit of its natural management objectives for Yellowstone, and to protect its living communities and all that they represent, the Park Service employs a professional, highly competent and dedicated staff of scientists and resource managers. Without their dedication some species may yet succumb to the finality of extinction. Sadly, the natural world grows smaller and less secure each day!

Left: A porcupine is seen clinging a tree. The second largest of our rodents after the beaver, the porcupine can be found in most forests of Yellowstone, but is often hard to find because of its mostly nocturnal activities.
Photo by Michael S. Quinton / Minden Pictures

Above: River otters are about 4 feet (1.20 m) long, brown, with short legs and webbed feet. Playful and active, they feed mostly on fish, which they catch with speed and agility. They often "ice-fish" in winter and benefit from a fur well adapted to the cold, with long guard hairs and dense, wavy underfur. Sebaceous glands secrete oil, waterproofing the fur and protecting the skin from frigid water.
Photo by Michael S. Quinton / Minden Pictures

SMALLER CREATURES

True to the nature's economic structure, where small things are of value, there are millions of very small creatures in the park playing their important role in the overall ecological health of the park. Copepods (small crustaceans) and other zooplankton living in Yellowstone's waters, as well as millions of insects are all near the bottom of many food chains.

Insects are responsible for the greatest diversity among park invertebrates with 12,000 species of insects, ranging from aphids to wasps, having been observed. Nearly 120 species of butterflies, including the rare Yellowstone checkerspot, add bright, flickering spots of color to the air. Common "painted ladies," as some butterflies have been called, include: anise swallowtails, western sulphurs, checkered whites, lupine blues, blue coppers, sylvan hairstreaks, variegated fritillaries, mourning cloaks, monarchs, and others.

Reptiles and amphibians are also present in the park, although in small numbers. Cold blooded, they have to absorb much of their body heat from the environment in which they live. The long cold winters and the overall dry conditions of the park limit their population to only four known amphibians, and six reptile species.

The prairie rattlesnake is the only dangerous venomous snake in the park. Present in drier and warmer areas of Yellowstone, it is a large-bodied snake, reaching a length of about 4 feet (1.20m), with a tail ending in a rattle. Its color varies from greenish gray, to greenish brown or light brown with darker blotches. The valley garter snake, the wandering garter snake, the bullsnake, and the rubber boa, related to pythons and boa constrictors, are also found. The sagebrush lizard which can grow to 5 inches (12 cm), is the only lizard present in Yellowstone.

There are only four species of amphibians in the park. The boreal chorus frog, the Columbia spotted frog, the boreal toad, and the tiger salamander. Their exact numbers in the park are not known but their numbers are thought to be declining as in other

parts of the West. As amphibians live both in water and on land, they are highly sensitive to the deterioration of the health of any environments at many levels.

The Columbia spotted frog is the most abundant and best-known amphibian in Yellowstone. It is found all summer throughout the park where water is available.

Above: A group of greenish blue butterflies. There are more than 12,000 species of insects listed in the park, including the mysterious ephydrid fly living near the park's hot springs and in waters as hot as 109°F (43°C).
Photo by Tom Murphy

Left: A nest of prairie rattlesnakes. This snake is one of only six reptile species present in the park. Although dangerous, its bite is usually not fatal and only two bites have been recorded in the entire park history.
Photo by Jeff Henry

The Fish of Yellowstone

Fed by rain and mostly snow, the waters of Yellowstone include more than 500 streams, 124 of them feeding Yellowstone Lake, and 150 lakes covering about five percent of the park's surface. These waters, including the headwaters of three major North American rivers: the Missouri, Columbia, and Colorado, provide rich and diverse habitats for aquatic life.

Yellowstone waters create unique, fragile and often unseen worlds of living organisms, each with their own elaborate food chains. Plants and decaying plant matter support the plant eaters, bacteria, plankton, and insects, all serving as a foundation supporting a world of progressively larger predators. Small fish are eaten by larger fish which become the target of other predators such as dippers, pelicans, ospreys, eagles, herons, raccoons, otters, and bears.

Humans, of course, play their part in the complex food chains, by their influence on this fragile world with pollution, habitat destruction and introduction of non-native species, and as predators themselves. In recent years, as many as 75,000 anglers a year have flocked to the park's waters from around the world to test their skills in one of the greatest trout fisheries found anywhere.

Since the melting of the last glaciers in the area, Yellowstone's waters have slowly become suitable habitat for 12 native species of fish including Yellowstone, westslope, and Snake River fine-spotted cutthroat trout, arctic grayling, mountain whitefish, longnose dace, speckled dace, redside shiner, Utah chub, mottled sculpin, and the longnose sucker.

The Yellowstone Cutthroat Trout *(Oncorhynchus clarki bouvieri)*

Before the arrival of the white man and the establishment of Yellowstone National Park only about 40% of the park waters had established fish populations. Freed from the thick cover of ice for about 12,000 to 14,000 years, a short time in geological and ecological terms, some stream stretches above waterfalls, isolated water drainages and lakes, had remained naturally fishless, because of natural barriers to fish movement. Yet, where fish populations were established their numbers were extraordinary and at the time of the first explorations into the Yellowstone area and the arrival of the first tourists, fishing was nothing more than an exercise in pulling as many fish out of water as fast as possible!

After the establishment of the park, with a slow and steady increase in visitation, park managers decided to populate fishless waters and better provide for the "enjoyment of the people" by beginning an intensive stocking program throughout the park. Native and non-native species, such as rainbow trout, brook trout, and brown trout were introduced to many of the park waters. The lake trout was also introduced into fishless Lewis Lake in the 1880s.

With the creation of the National Park Service in 1916 and the evolution of a new ecological approach to wildlife and park management, fish stocking practices progressively came to an end and by 1936 non-native fish stocking was abandoned altogether.

Unfortunately, increased visitation, high creel limits, and over-harvesting of cutthroat eggs for stocking purposes, continued to diminish the resource and nearly destroyed the fishery in many areas of the park by the 1960s.

In response to this crisis new regulations and the development of progressive fisheries management policies were focused on three important principles: first, *"to manage aquatic resources as an important part of the park ecosystem;"* second, *"to preserve and restore native fishes and their habitats;"* and finally, *"to provide recreational fishing opportunities for the enjoyment of park visitors, consistent with the first two objectives."* These principles are to be followed in an environment where *"bald eagles, ospreys, pelicans, otters, grizzly bears, and other wildlife take precedence over humans in utilizing fish as food."*

Gradually, creel limits were reduced and catch-and-release-only policies were enacted for the Yellowstone cutthroat in the 1970s. Finally in 2001, all native sport species in the entire park were put under catch-and-release-only fishing rules. These policies have helped the population of native fish, especially the cutthroat populations, to rebound quite dra-

The Westlope Cutthroat Trout *(Oncorhynchus clarki lewisi)*

matically in many areas of Yellowstone.

Preserving the aquatic resources of the park is an important ongoing fight as new threats jeopardize the ecological health of the Greater Yellowstone area. For example, as recently as 1994, the discovery of lake trout in Yellowstone Lake has alarmed biologists because lake trout aggressively prey on Yellowstone Cutthroats. Called "an appalling act of environmental vandalism" this illegal introduction, if left uncontrolled, could seriously deplete or eliminate the native cutthroat population which represent as much as 80% of the lake trout's diet. Studies done in other places indicate that a single lake trout may account for the loss of as many as 60 cutthroat trout a year. This could

The Snake River Finespotted Cutthroat Trout *(Oncorhynchus clarki behnkei)*

The Arctic (Montana) Grayling *(Thymallus arcticus)*

The Mountain Whitefish *(Prosopium williamsoni)*

have far-reaching ecological effects on other species. Cutthroat trout are an important food source for more than 40 species of birds and animals in the park and beyond. Species that would be adversely affected include ospreys, eagles, pelicans, river otters, and grizzly bears that rely heavily on spawning cutthroats for food. To control this threat, resource managers have begun an aggressive gillnetting program and anglers have been asked to destroy each lake trout taken. Fisheries biologists hope that these measures will help maintain the native cutthroat trout population at levels that will not affect species relying on them for food.

All illustrations © Joseph R. Tomelleri

HISTORY

Humans were probably not present in the Greater Yellowstone region when the entire area was covered by ice, a time that ended approximately 14,000 years ago. When the ice receded, it left behind rivers and valleys that people and animals could follow. The first people are thought to have arrived in this region sometime before 10,000 years ago. They were likely nomadic big-game hunters who had followed large mammals into the region. They hunted species now extinct such as the wooly mammoth, giant sloths, and camels, but also pursued species that we know well today such as the bison, elk, deer, bighorn sheep, and bears. Archaeologists have found little physical evidence of their presence other than their distinctive stone tools and projectile points. Scientists studying these artifacts believe that these early people hunted mammals but also ate berries, seeds, and roots. These early visitors were the first in a long procession of people drawn to the Yellowstone region. They were harbingers of a time, still thousands of years away, when nearly a quarter of a million of their descendants would live in or near the Greater Yellowstone Ecosystem, and when three million others, would come to it each year.

By about 7,000 years ago, when the climate slowly warmed and dried, these new residents slowly adapted to the changing conditions of their environment and to the disappearance of some of their game. As the larger animals became scarce and disappeared, early hunters could not rely on them as prey. Instead smaller game such as deer and bighorn sheep became important in their diet, along with plants such as bitterroot and prickly pear. Evidence of

The beaver was always a very important animal in the ecological development of the west. Working to create a safe environment for its family, the beaver creates large dams and ponds. These ponds, after time, develop into marshes and bogs and finally into meadows. These meadows in turn attract large deer and their predators: wolves, bears and mountain lions. Beavers, with their expensive pelts, also played a critical role in the "discovery" of the West by white trappers and settlers. The pelts constituted the economic incentive to explore valleys, mountain ranges, and new water drainages.
Photo by Jeff Foott

those early humans and the groups that followed is abundant. Projectile points and the flaky debris from their manufacture, evidence of the quarrying and widespread distribution of volcanic glass (obsidian) for arrow and spear points, and habitation sites, all present a clear record of their presence in the area over a long period. (See sidebar)

The arrival of the white man in the region was led by French Canadian trappers of the 18th century who wandered through much of the Intermountain West, but they are not known to have entered Yellowstone or to have seen the thermal features. They did travel the reaches of the upper Missouri River and its tributaries, including a river that they called the "riviere des roches jaunes" or "river of yellow stones." That name, given to them by a tribe of Minnetaree Indians who lived near the lower river, originated from the words "Mi tse a-da-zi" for the yellow-colored bluffs near present-day Billings, Montana.

As the new America was taking shape and after the Louisiana Purchase from France in 1803, Thomas Jefferson sent Meriwether Louis and William Clark on a fantastic military expedition through the American West all the way to the Pacific Northwest. The expedition successfully achieved their goal by mapping and reporting on this vast new territory. On their return trip, after two-and-a-half years, the expedition was back on the Missouri when John Colter, a mountain man and trapper, asked permission to leave the expedition to join trappers in the area and further explore this region for furs and possible trading with the local tribes.

During his travel in the area and especially while meandering during the winter of 1807-08,

Preceding pages: Soda Butte Creek, in the upper Lamar Valley. The wide sweeping views of the Lamar Valley offer great vantage points to view wildlife. Bison, elk, pronghorn, moose, black bears, and grizzly bears, are often seen from the Northeast Entrance road. Early and late in the day, this area offers a very good chance to observe wolves.
Photo by Willard Clay

Left: The banks of the firehole river appear in the fog in what once was labeled "Colter's Hell." John Colter was probably the first white man to gaze upon the wonders of Yellowstone.
Photo by Carr Clifton

Right: Like trappers and explorers before him, wrangler C.T. Ripley is leading a pack string into the Thorofare region of Yellowstone. This area, in the southeast corner of the park, was named by fur trappers of the 1820s and 1830s as it represented the only known way into the Yellowstone Plateau from Jackson Hole. Native Americans before them had used this same approach for centuries.
Photo by Jeff Henry

The Native Americans

The human presence in the Rocky Mountains has been dated to between 10,000 and 8,000 B.C. Archaeologists have found evidence of several cultures that apparently evolved in response to changing climate, vegetation, and animal life. Those changes are partially inferred from changes in the type of projectile points used by hunters and suggest that over time different kinds of animals were hunted. Like geologists who read the rocks and chronicle the physical evolution of the place, archaeologists have divided the human record into temporal periods that they call cultures, each with characteristic artifacts. The presence of artifacts confirms a periodic human occupation in the region by various cultures since about 12,000 years ago. It is in the last few hundred years that the record is most complete, yet ample evidence exists from the earlier periods to know the Yellowstone region was inhabited.

Archaeologists have discovered obsidian flakes, wickiups, and other evidence of campsites throughout Yellowstone including in the Norris, Midway and Lower geyser basins. More than 400 former habitation sites have been documented, and more than 40 of them were in thermal basins. Campsites have been located around Mammoth Hot Springs, on the Bannock Trail, along the Firehole River, near Old Faithful, at Obsidian Cliff, at several spots around the shoreline of Yellowstone Lake, and elsewhere in the Greater Yellowstone Ecosystem. Mummy Cave is a rock shelter in the Absaroka Mountains west of Cody. Excavated from 1963 to 1966, the site is significant because it has 38 separate cultural layers or strata. Each layer is made up of the physical deposits left during a period of human occupation spanning 9,200 years. A human burial was found on Cultural Layer 3, providing the site with its name.

Recent fieldwork by archaeologists has revealed 9,400 year-old artifacts from a campsite at Osprey Beach. This site was occupied during the summer by the earliest know people to have lived on the shore of Yellowstone Lake. Centuries-old blood residue from rabbits, deer, bears, bighorn sheep, and unspecified dogs and cats was revealed by forensic analysis of projectile points found there.

The early hunters encamped at Osprey Beach are part of a cultural unit that archaeologists call the Cody Complex. They were previously thought to occupy only the plains and foothills and to subsist mainly on bison.

The variety of stone tools discovered at Osprey Beach, including knives, projectile points, shaft straighteners, scrapers, an adze (curved blade tool to shape wood), and others, indicate that domestic, repair, and manufacturing activities took place at the site. Since the bow and arrow did not appear until about A.D. 200, the projectile points were probably attached to spears or darts. Archaeologists believe that the campsite was occupied for days or weeks at a time.

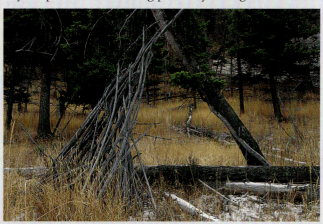

Several hundred archeological sites have been discovered along the Yellowstone River valley and on the shoreline of Yellowstone Lake. Sites (including one from the Cody Complex) have also been found on six of the seven islands in the lake, but there is still no evidence of how the occupants might have reached the sites during the summer. Archaeologists speculate that the abundance of game and other resources, such as ample water and obsidian for tools and weapons, probably attracted pre-European contact people to the Yellowstone area.

Members of several "modern" American Indian tribes are known to have entered Yellowstone during the past two hundred years, especially after they acquired the horse from Spanish Conquistadors. Among the tribes that have connections with the area are the Blackfoot, Crow, Shoshone-Bannock, and the Nez Perce. In addition to material evidence such as tipi rings and wickiups, Native American presence is documented in the journals of early mountain men and explorers such as Jim Bridger, Osborne Russell, and members of the Washburn-Langford expedition.

The Bannocks were a group of the Northern Paiute living peacefully among the Shoshone. One of the prominent travel routes across the Yellowstone country is the famous Bannock Trail, which was used by the Bannocks and others as they sought bison on the eastern high plains. Bison were gone from the Snake River Plains to the west by the 1840s. The Bannock Indians followed a 200-mile-long route across the northern part of Yellowstone to reach the remaining herds in the Bighorn Basin and Powder River country east of the mountains. Their route was known as the Bannock Trail, a rough route beginning in Camas Meadows in central Idaho through the northern end of Yellowstone and onto the Clark's Fork and Shoshone Rivers in northern Wyoming.

Many different native people, including hunters from the Northern Shoshone, Nez Perce, Salish, Pend d'Oreille, and Crow tribes, used the trail for thousands of years. A lengthy portion of the trail extends through the Tower District from the Blacktail Plateau to where it crosses the Yellowstone River at the Bannock Ford upstream from Tower Creek. From the river, the trail's main fork ascends the Lamar River splitting at Soda Butte Creek. From there, one fork ascends the creek before leaving the park. Traces of the trail can still be plainly seen in various locations, particularly on the Blacktail Plateau and at the Lamar-Soda Butte confluence.

Left: A family of Sheepeater Indians. Part of the Shoshone group, they were named after their principal food source, the bighorn sheep. In 1835, the trapper Osborne Russell recorded in his journal an encounter with a band of Sheepeaters and described them to be : "...well armed with bows and arrows pointed with obsidian. The bows were beautifully wrought from sheep, buffaloe and elk horns..." He also observed that they were all neatly clothed in dressed deer and sheepskins of the best quality and seemed to be perfectly contented and happy.
Photo NPS Historic Photo Collection

Above: Native Americans found refuge in simple, but strong, pole and hide shelters called "wickiups." The vestigial remains of wickiups can still be found scattered throughout the park.
Photo NPS Historic Photo Collection

The Shoshone referred to individual tribal bands by the principal food of the group. Thus, within the larger tribe there were Buffalo Eaters, Salmon Eaters, Rabbit Eaters, and Sheepeaters. The Sheepeaters were the only long-term Indian occupants in the park.

Trappers and explorers first reported the presence of Sheepeaters in the Yellowstone area around 1800. They described numbers of about 400 altogether in 15 camp groups. The sheepeaters probably arrived in the park as part of the slow, general migration of tribes across the Great Basin toward the northeast and lived in the region for only about 100 years. They moved their small encampments from high in the mountains in the summer to the lower elevations in winter, adjusting to the seasonal movements of bighorn sheep and the availability of other foods such as small game, berries, nuts, fish, plant roots, ants, and grubs. Sheepeaters depended largely on sheep for their livelihood. They hunted the sheep with intricately woven juniper fiber nets, traps with drivelines and sheep-horn bows.

Sheepeater homes were either simple domed wickiups made of loosely stacked poles and brush, covered with animal hides, or were roofless shelters made of a semi-circle of poles with branches piled against them. They used rocks, the hand-shaped mano and flat metate, to grind seeds and nuts into a kind of flour that they mixed and cooked in stone pots. Heavy and cumbersome, the stone implements were often left in the campsite, cached for future use.

The Sheepeaters' clothing was made of soft, finely tanned hides of deer, elk, and bighorn sheep. They used stone knives, scrapers, fire-hardened digging sticks, and they made highly prized bows from animal horns and antlers. Their beautifully tanned hides and horn bows were sometimes traded with other tribes.

Sadly, by 1882, most of the Sheepeaters had gone to various reservations because of treaties that excluded them and other tribes from the newly created park.

While some native people may have avoided the more active geothermal features, evidence doesn't indicate that Indians were fearful of these areas. In fact, campsites have been found near some of them. There is some indication that they may have believed that the "steaming waters that go up and down," were manifestations of powerful spirits (neither good nor bad) that could be summoned to their aid by prayer. Warriors may have sought them on vision quests. In any case, there is no reason to believe that these first visitors were any more, or less, awed by the geysers and other features than visitors are today.

Colorful, and often embellished, accounts of mountain men were probably responsible for the early assumption that Native Americans were fearful of Yellowstone's thermal features. One such account, from the journal of trapper Warren Ferris, attributes the statement "Hell must be in the vicinity," to a Pend d'Oreille Indian guide accompanying him to features along the Firehole River in 1834. A journalist recounting John Colter's trek into Yellowstone in the early 1800s, called the place "Colter's Hell," and Jim Bridger said it was a place "where hell bubbled up." Still, hundreds of years before the first Euro-Americans witnessed the geothermal features, Native Americans probably visited geyser basins and likely had a healthy respect for the dangers of the area. Yellowstone country was revered and accorded a sacred place in the world view of most tribes. The Shoshone and Bannock tribes (and probably others) believed that powerful spirits were associated with Yellowstone's geothermal features. They came to Yellowstone on vision quests, hoping that the spirits would grant them "good medicine." The cultural traditions of various tribes involved the use of hot springs for bathing and cooking, the use of mud to clean the skin, and pigments to make paint. Sheepeaters may have soaked bighorn horns in hot water to make them malleable enough to shape into their prized bows..

Tribes that are known to have often traveled to Yellowstone include the Nez Perce, Flathead, Kalispell, Pen d'Oreille, and Coeur dAlene. The Assiniboine may have traveled to the region from the plains of northeastern Montana, and some references suggest that the Arapaho and Lakota Sioux occasionally visited too. The Shoshone called Yellowstone the place where "water keeps coming out." The Blackfoot called it "many smokes." Other tribes referred to Yellowstone country as "burning mountain," and "summit of the world."

The 1877 flight of Chief Joseph and his band followed a route through Yellowstone too. Born in 1840 in the Wallowa Valley in what is now northeastern Oregon, Joseph was named "Hin-mah-tooyah-lat-kekt" which means "Thunder Rolling Down the Mountain," he became a chief when his father, the elder Joseph, died in 1871.

General Oliver Otis Howard ordered the Nez Perce, the tribe called themselves Nimiipu, to a reservation in 1877. The Nez Perce refused to go. Instead, Chief Joseph tried to lead 800 of his people on a 1,400-mile march to Canada, which included a crossing of the northern part of Yellowstone. They were trapped just 40 miles from the Canadian border. After a five-day fight, the remaining 431 Nez Perce surrendered in September 1877. Chief Joseph then made his famous speech in which he said, *"I will fight no more forever."* General William Tecumseh Sherman said that Joseph's flight, and engagements with 2,000 soldiers, was one of the most brilliant military retreats in American history.

Right: The plain Shoshone had a horse-mounted bison-hunting culture. Although they remained in the plains, where game was more plentiful, they more likely travelled through and knew of Yellowstone. It is believed that the last of the Sheepeaters may have joined the Wind River band of the Shoshone by the early 1880s. This photo of Chief Washakie's Band was taken by William Henry Jackson during the 1870 Hayden Expedition near Sweetwater River, Wyoming.
Photo NPS Hist. Photo Collection

Above: Chief Joseph led a band of 800 Nez Perce people across northern Yellowstone on their famous, but unsuccessful flight to Canada in 1877. They wanted to join Sitting Bull, victor against Custer, instead of being forced to reservation life.
Photo NPS Hist. Photo Collection

History

John Colter is believed to have become the first white man to see the wonders of Yellowstone. Indeed, upon his return to St. Louis in 1810, he is said to have conferred with William Clark on what he had seen and his observations were included in maps published in 1840 as part of Clark's overall report. These included descriptions of the Yellowstone River, Yellowstone Lake (then called Eustis Lake), and one thermal area named "Hot Spring Brimstone."

Colter was soon followed into the region by other hardy mountain men in the 1820s and 30s, among them Joe Meek and Jim Bridger, who spent three years trapping in Yellowstone country. When Bridger returned to St. Louis with tales of a "place where hell bubbled up," his stories were labeled "preposterous." While he probably embellished a bit, as storytelling mountain men were wont to do, his descriptions of places like Obsidian Cliff, Alum Creek, the Firehole River, and other landmarks were not so far-fetched.

Joe Meek, Osborne Russell, and Daniel Potts were among the first trappers to spend time in the Yellowstone region. Through the jour-

nals of Osborne Russell, who spent nine years roaming the region between 1834 and 1843, we are able to glimpse what the Yellowstone country was like more than 150 years ago. Russell was a keen observer of the land and the life of the times. Often writing in unschooled but surprisingly literate form, he was nonetheless a sensitive and articulate writer who painted vivid verbal images of Yellowstone. His journals include some of the earliest descriptions of the fauna, including the gray wolf, as well as character sketches of the Shoshone and Crow Indians. In his work *Journal of a Trapper*, Russell said of the Lamar Valley: *"There is something in the wild romantic scenery of this valley which I cannot nor will I, attempt to describe but the impressions made upon my mind while gazing from a high eminence on the surrounding landscape one evening as the sun was gently gliding behind the western mountain and casting its gigantic shadows across the vale were such as time can never efface from my memory..."*

Joe Meek had a way with words too. In describing a geyser basin he said: *"...and behold! The whole country beyond was smoking with vapor from boiling springs; and burning with gases issuing from small*

Above left: William Henry Jackson (1843-1942) was the first to photograph Old Faithful in eruption during the Hayden Expedition of 1871.
NPS Hist. Photo Collection

Above: A possible image of Thomas Moran, famed painter, at Mammoth Hot Springs taken by William Henry Jackson in 1871.
NPS Hist. Photo Collection

Left: Thomas Moran joined the Hayden expedition of 1871 and depicted the wonders of Yellowstone in some of the better known paintings of the national parks. His dramatic work influenced others to visit, and advocate the protection of Yellowstone.
Smithsonian Amer. Art Mus. Wash. DC/ Art Resource NY

craters, each of which was emitting a sharp, whistling sound."

By about 1840, the near elimination of beaver populations in the Intermountain West, and the increasing popularity of the silk hat which destroyed the demand for fine beaver felt, signaled the end of the trapping era. While in earlier years the possibility of finding a rich source of pelts had attracted trappers to the region, for the next 20 years the area remained the domain of the Indian, only rarely visited by others.

People searching for precious metals followed the trappers

during the 1860s. Caught up in the frenzy over the rich Montana gold strike of 1862, prospectors, entered the area. Finding none of the alluring metal, they nevertheless provided more information on the region. One of them, Walter W. DeLacy, published the first relatively accurate map of the Yellowstone area in 1865, two years after his party's unsuccessful prospecting foray.

Other efforts were also being made in the early 1860s to further explore and map the Yellowstone country. The first organized attempt was mounted in the fall of 1860 when a small expedition, under the leadership of Army Captain William F. Raynolds, and guided by Jim Bridger, attempted to enter the area but failed to go very far because of early and heavy snow. More and better organized expeditions by other parties were put on hold as the country was in the midst of a terrible civil war.

Determined to see for themselves the wonders that had been described by earlier mountain men, local residents, David E. Folsom, Charles W. Cook, and William Peterson entered the area in 1869 for an extensive 36-day wilderness trip. They saw most of what Colter, Bridger, and DeLacy had seen, and much more. They explored extensively and produced a much-improved version of DeLacy's 1865 map. Upon their return Folsom and Cook wrote an article recounting their adventure which was published by the Chicago magazine *Western Monthly*, after being rejected by other periodicals as "unreliable" for the wonders described.

Their interest stirred by the recollections of the Folsom-Cook-Peterson adventures, a group of several prominent residents of the Montana Territory decided to mount an expedition of their own in 1870 with Surveyor General Henry D. Washburn as the leader. Nathaniel P. Langford, (later to become the first superintendent of the new park), Cornelius Hedges, and Truman Everts, along with a military escort under the command of Lieutenant Gustavus C. Doane, were also part of what became known as the Washburn Expedition.

Above: Harry Yount, nicknamed "Rocky Mountain Harry" was a guide during the 1874 Hayden Expedition and had a deep knowledge of the area. He was later hired by Philetus W. Norris as a guard to repel poachers and vandals and thus became known as the first national park ranger.
NPS Historic Photograph Collection

Above right: The Hayden Expedition of 1870 led Ferdinand V. Hayden (seen sitting at middle table) into the Wyoming territory. In 1871, as head of the U.S Geological Survey, he lead the first official exploration of Yellowstone. His reports were crucial in the establishment of Yellowstone National Park in 1872.
NPS Historic Photograph Collection

Right: The Firehole River at sunset in the Midway Geyser Basin. The colors, fumes, and the amazing sense of wonder impressed the first visitors to Yellowstone so much that they began to lobby Congress, immediately upon their return, to set the area apart in perpetuity for the benefit of all people.
Photo by Tim Fitzharris

History

This expedition traveled extensively through the features of the Upper, Midway, and Lower Geyser basins and descended in the Grand Canyon of the Yellowstone. Its members were so taken by the sheer beauty and uniqueness of the features that they began naming them. A regularly erupting geyser was thus named "Old Faithful."

Popular tradition suggests that the idea of creating a park for the "benefit of all people" was born in a discussion at a campfire near the junction of the Firehole and Gibbon rivers during this expedition, but there is uncertainty about that meeting, its location, and the individual motives of the participants. The plans of railroad financier Jay Cooke to extend the Northern Pacific Railroad lines to within 50 miles of Yellowstone's wonders, and the immense potential for profit from tourism were almost certainly known to members of the Washburn-Langford-Doane party that September evening. Yet, Cornelius Hedges, a young lawyer from Helena, Montana, is credited with suggesting that the group disavow personal interests and advocate that the Yellowstone country be preserved for the benefit of all people. While discussions among the men may not have been entirely altruistic, nonetheless, they ultimately led to future exploration, discovery, and the establishment of Yellowstone National Park.

Reports from the explorations of 1869 and 1870, a speaking tour by Langford taking him to the East and the Capital, numerous newspaper articles, and a story in the popular *Scribner's Monthly* contributed to the increasing body of knowledge and folklore about this western wonderland. The official report written by Lt. Doane was also accepted and published by Congress.

The growing publicity finally resulted in the United States government funding and supporting an official exploration in 1871. Ferdinand V. Hayden, head of the U.S. Geological Survey, was to lead the large expedition. Hayden's purpose was to explore the region thoroughly and scientifically. To do this he assembled a party of scientists and asked noted photographer William Henry Jackson and artists Thomas Moran and Henry W. Elliott to provide a visual record. The United States Army Corps of Engineers was to complement their findings with a simultaneous survey.

Thomas Moran first saw Yellowstone during this expedition, but a few months earlier had already reworked sketches submitted as illustrations for an article on Yellowstone published in *Scribner's* magazine. That article, "The

Above left: In 1877, Philetus W. Norris became the first paid superintendent of the new park. He also benefited from the first budget of $10,000 appropriated by Congress in 1877 to "protect, preserve, and improve the park." He is seen here (second from right) during an 1878 expedition into the upper Fire Hole Basin with his party.
NPS Historic Photograph Collection

Above: One of the first groups of tourists to visit Yellowstone at Mammoth Hot Springs in 1876.
Library of Congress / NPS Historic Photograph Collection

Left: In August 1886, 50 soldiers of the First United States Cavalry from Fort Custer, Montana Territory entered Yellowstone and set up at Mammoth Hot Springs to bring order to the management of the park. These troops are from 1st. U.S. Cavalry, at Fort Yellowstone, early 1900s.
NPS Historic Photograph Collection

Wonders of Yellowstone," had been the first extensive description published of the Yellowstone country. The field sketches, which Moran completed during the 1871 expedition, were the first color images of Yellowstone ever seen in the East. William Henry Jackson, a self-taught artist and photographer, became the first photographer to successfully capture the awe-inspiring features of the area on film and provided visual proof of their existence. Henry W. Elliott, also an artist, was a field correspondent for *Leslie's Illustrated*. He provided the magazine, widely read in the East, with vivid descriptions of the area, and all its spectacular features.

The Hayden expedition was a complete success, bringing back accurate field reports with collected specimens and visual records. Together they provided the world with confirmation that the wonders of Yellowstone did indeed exist.

Members of the Washburn and Hayden expeditions were so impressed with the spectacle offered by the place, that they were convinced it should somehow be preserved for others to see and enjoy. Hayden, together with members of the Washburn party and others, albeit probably influenced by the commercial tourism motives and interests of the Northern Pacific Railroad, lobbied tirelessly in 1871 and early 1872, for a congressional bill to protect Yellowstone.

Supported by Hayden's official report and following the precedent of the 1864 Act that made Yosemite Valley part of the public domain, Congress enacted the historic legislation: *"...to set apart a certain tract of land lying near the headwaters of the Yellowstone River as a public park."* The enabling legislation articulated: *"...that the tract of land in the Territories of Montana and Wyoming lying near the headwaters of the Yellowstone River, and described as... is hereby reserved and withdrawn from settlement, occupancy, or sale under the laws of the United States, and dedicated and set apart as a public park or pleasuring ground for the benefit and enjoyment of the people...."*

When President Ulysses S. Grant signed the bill on March 1, 1872, Yellowstone became the world's first national park, ensuring that future generations would forever find its incredible features unimpaired.

As the park was formed it quickly became clear that without an infrastructure or a blueprint of any kind, it would be very difficult to manage the new entity and to make good on the promises of protection for the benefit and enjoyment of the people. Congress, in all its wisdom, had actually not planned to set aside any money for the management of the park and was hoping that it could manage itself, without any cost to the government. It was argued that money would be provided for the development of the area by the Northern Pacific Railroad, by the new concessionaires, and by the thousands of tourists who would flock to visit the natural wonders of Yellowstone. Nevertheless, the park was placed under the direction of the Secretary of the Interior who named a superintendent in 1872 to oversee the management of the park.

The first superintendent selected was Nathaniel P. Langford. His

Above right: A 1904 party of tourist having their "laundry" done in what became known as Handkerchief Pool. This pool, located in the Black Sand Basin of the Upper Geyser Basin, is now filled with sinter.
NPS Historic Photograph Collection

Above: A soldier stationed in Yellowstone, to defend the park from poachers and vandals, explains to one of the early 1903 tourists how a geyser works. The uniform worn today by national park rangers is a direct tribute to these first "soldier rangers."
NPS Historic Photograph Collection

Right: The Yellowstone Lake Hotel was initially constructed in 1891, with additions made in 1902, 1904, and 1923. The Lake Hotel was the first large scale hotel to be built to accommodate the largely wealthy clientele and was host to presidents Harding and Coolidge as they visited the park. Seen here in 1905 as visitors ready themselves for an excursion through Yellowstone in "stagecoach" style carriages.
Photo by William Henry Jackson / NPS Historic Photograph Collection

History

unpaid position, without much clout or power to manage the huge tract of land, as large as the state of Maryland and Delaware combined, failed to give Langford any chances for much success in his work. As political pressure mounted and abuses of the parks resources became obvious, such as mass hunting and poaching of park animals, destruction of geological features by souvenir hunters, and outright greed displayed by uncontrolled would-be concessionaires, the Secretary of the Interior decided to fire Langford in 1877 and replace him with Philetus W. Norris. Norris thus became the parks first paid superintendent and armed with a modest salary and a budget of $10,000 a year authorized by Congress, he took on the task of protecting and slowly transforming the park.

Curbing the rampant poaching and vandalism in the new park was high on Norris's priority list. To patrol, and possibly police, the vast expanses of Yellowstone, Norris hired Harry Yount ("Rocky Mountain Harry"), who had worked as a wrangler and packer for the Hayden Survey. Unfortunately, alone there is not much he could have achieved for the park and after many months of frustration Yount decided to resign. In his resignation letter Yount wrote: *"I do not think that any one man . . . is what is needed or can prove effective for certain necessary purposes, but a small and reliable police force of men... is what is really the most practicable way of seeing that the game is protected from wanton slaughter, the forests from careless use of fire, and the enforcement of all the other laws, rules, and regulations for the protection and improvement of the park."* Yount's words were an augury of an organization that would not take shape for 35 years. While Yount was hired as the park's first "gamekeeper," he is now honored as the first National Park Ranger.

The passenger department of the Northern Pacific Railroad was instrumental in the early history of the park. The railroad funded the development of several large hotels, including the defunct National Hotel at Mammoth Hot Springs, and the Old Faithful Inn, near the main features. It produced a series of colorful and informative guidebooks and posters, and enthusiastically

promoted the park, urging its expansion and the protection of its resources. The company became one of the most outspoken and influential supporters of the park and its preservation.

The Northern Pacific provided access to the new park by laying a spur line south from Livingston, Montana, to the railroad's station at Gardiner, Montana. Most early park visitors arrived via rail, disembarked at Gardiner, and rode stagecoaches, later supplanted by open-topped tour buses, to park

Above left: The historical Roosevelt arch at the park's north entrance near Gardiner Montana. This arch, dedicated by President Theodore Roosevelt on April 24, 1903 is engraved with the words; "For the benefit and enjoyment of the people."
Photo by Jeff Henry

Above: Horace Albright became the first "professionally trained" superintendent of Yellowstone and served in this position from 1919 to 1929. He followed Stephen T. Mather as head of the National Park Service in 1929 and stayed in this position until his retirement in 1933. He is seen here with a baby elk raised by rangers at Mammoth Hot Springs.
NPS Historic Photograph Collection

Left: One of the very first cars to enter Yellowstone National Park is seen here on Aug. 1, 1915. The arrival of the car revolutionized the popularity of national parks and swelled the number of visitors.
Haynes Foundation Coll. courtesy NPS Historic Photograph Collection

hotels and features. In fact, most of today's paved roads follow early stage routes. Mammoth Hot Springs became the logical focal point for park administration and early visitor use due to its proximity to rail access.

As might be expected with an entirely new type of public land, the earliest attempts at park administration were underfunded, disorganized, and largely ineffective. Although Norris managed to expand the road and trail network within the park and the access to many of its features, the park's resources continued to be abused. Norris was fired, and a succession of superintendent who followed could not achieve much better. Because of conflicts arising from the need to develop tourist facilities and the demands of concessionaires for exclusive privileges and rights, and the increasing numbers of settlers who simply took possession of land without permits or leases, a state of chaos reigned in the park. Very frustrated, Congress cancelled all funding to the park and asked the Secretary of War for help. The Care of Yellowstone had officially been entrusted to the United States Army. In August 1886, fifty soldiers of Company M, 1st U.S. Cavalry from Fort Custer of the Montana Territory, arrived at Mammoth Hot Springs and became the official custodians of the world's first national park.

The troops began to work on creating "order out of chaos," patrolling the four corners of the park year-round and in all weather, on horseback and skis, and manning new army-built soldier stations and patrol cabins in the wilderness. While poaching remained a problem for a while, it finally came under control after the passage by Congress of the National Park Protection Act (the Lacey Act) in 1894, giving protection to birds and animals in Yellowstone.

During the ensuing 30 years, the army accomplished much. They improved access to the park, constructed facilities, protected its features and forests, apprehended poachers and stage robbers, and made early visitors more secure.

With the establishment of a public park came the need for public and administrative facilities. The U.S. Army constructed Camp Sheridan at the base of Capitol Hill at Mammoth Hot Springs when it began to manage the park. Camp Sheridan was gradually replaced by the many buildings of Fort Yellowstone, most of which are still in use by the National Park Service; the Albright Visitor Center was the bachelor officer's quarters, and the Park Headquarters was the cavalry barracks. Scottish masons did the exceptional stonework in many of those buildings.

Several noted architects, Robert C. Reamer principal among them, contributed to the evolution of the unique and varied architectural styles of historic structures in Yellowstone. Prominent structures such as the Roosevelt Arch, Old Faithful Inn and Old Faithful Lodge, Hamilton's stores, Norris Soldier Station, the Norris, Madison and Lake museums, the buildings of Fort Yellowstone at Mammoth Hot Springs, and many others are among their legacies. Many of the park structures have the massive, rough-hewn, native timber and rock architectural signature common to the early western parks.

The first known tourist group of six men entered Yellowstone in August 1871, with the intention of following the route of the 1870 Washburn-Langford-Doane Expedition, but larger numbers of visitors did not begin to come to Yellowstone until the amenities provided by the railroad were completed. However, the number of tourists arriving in the park increased every year, with 5,000 tourists

Above right: The "Lunch Counter" where visitors could be treated to watching bears being fed refuse as an attraction. Not one of the smartest policies ever instituted by the park, it later contributed to bear management problems. Today, visitors are restricted from feeding any wildlife for their safety as well as for the animals' welfare.
NPS Historic Photograph Collection

Above: Stephen T. Mather was instrumental in the creation of the National Park Service, authorized by law in 1916, and became its first director until 1928.
NPS Historic Photograph Collection

Right: Ranger Frazier is seen here taking care of a herd of 15 bison at Mammoth Hot Springs in 1923. The bison population of Yellowstone was brought back from the brink when in 1902 only 50 remained. Twenty-one additional animals were brought in from outside the park and corralled at the Buffalo Ranch in Hayden Valley (now site of the Yellowstone Institute). They were successfully bred and released in the wild. There are now more than 3,500 bison in the park.
NPS Historic Photograph Collection

History

making the often very long and arduous journey in 1883 alone.

Noted British author Rudyard Kipling who traveled to the park in 1889, as well as other largely wealthy people, was among the increasing number of curious visitors seeking to confirm the tales of a western "wonderland" described in the Northern Pacific publications. Kipling's colorful language conjures vivid and differing images of Yellowstone: *"We drifted on, up that miraculous valley. On either side of us were hills from a thousand or fifteen hundred feet high, wooded from crest to heel. As far as the eye could range forward were columns of steam in the air, misshapen lumps of lime, mistlike preadamite monsters, still pools of turquoise-blue stretches of blue corn-flowers, a river that coiled on itself twenty times, pointed bowlders of strange colors, and ridges of glaring, staring white."*

The early 1900s brought growth to the young National Park System. In 1904 more than 100,000 people visited parks and monuments and by 1916, 360,000 visitors travelled to the 14 national parks and 21 national monuments already in existence. In Yellowstone alone the numbers of visitors had increased significantly especially after automobile travel in the park was authorized in 1915. The car had "democratized" the park experience and tourists freed from expensive hotels and train travel were now flocking to the great outdoors.

Then Secretary of the Interior Franklin K. Lane urged members of Congress to establish a separate agency, dedicated exclusively to the protection of the growing National Park System. On August 25, 1916, President Woodrow Wilson signed the National Park Service Act. The National Park Service, first conceived by Harry Yount in 1881 was thus created and Stephen T. Mather was appointed as its first director.

In Yellowstone, while there had been two designated superintendents, the new service relieved the successful army custodians and

Above: A pair of cross-country skiers enjoy the beauty offered by a winter trek among the steaming geysers of the Lower Geyser Basin. With nordic skis and snowshoes, winter explorers are able to blend in areas of the park without a sound to truly enjoy the marvels of the frozen stillness.
Photo by Jeff Henry

Above right: Midway Geyser Basin in the middle of the winter. The cold temperatures of winter, usually well below freezing, contrast with the steaming geothermal features to create amazing displays of steam, ice formations, and ice-covered "ghost trees."
Photo by Marc Muench

assumed responsibilities in 1918. A year later, Horace M. Albright, who would later succeed Mather as Director of the National Park Service, became the first in a long series of professionally trained, dedicated, and influential park managers serving as superintendent of Yellowstone: The World's First National Park.

The creation and establishment of Yellowstone is, perhaps, even more significant as a philosophical milestone than as an act of preservation. Yellowstone is ideologically linked with many disparate places around the globe. Like a river of ideas, the national park concept that took shape in the Yellowstone country more than 130 years ago has spread outward from its "headwaters," across the oceans, into a worldwide "watershed."

Like water, the national park concept touches all parts of the world and its people. Each year nearly 3 million visitors from many different nations flow into Yellowstone. Of course, they visit other places, other national parks, but coming to Yellowstone has special significance, because it is where it all began. For this reason, everything that happens in Yellowstone is in some way an historical event.

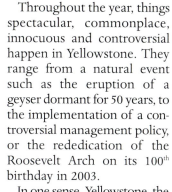

Throughout the year, things spectacular, commonplace, innocuous and controversial happen in Yellowstone. They range from a natural event such as the eruption of a geyser dormant for 50 years, to the implementation of a controversial management policy, or the rededication of the Roosevelt Arch on its 100th birthday in 2003.

In one sense, Yellowstone, the place and the idea, is a never-ending experiment.

In the 1940s wolves were considered "bad animals" and removed from the park by government hunters. Fifty-five years later, the same government realized that wolves were an essential missing piece of the ecological puzzle and restored them to Yellowstone.

Below: Visitors to Yellowstone now number about 2.8 million annually. The visitation, although heaviest in the summer months, is spread throughout the year and continues during the coldest of winter days. Using snowmobiles and snowcoaches provided by concessionaires in and around the park, visitors are able to travel far within the park and to see how the bitter cold affects the life of all species. Here, a group of bison take advantage of the few degrees of additional warmth, provided by the hot springs of the West Thumb Geyser Basin on the edge of frozen Lake Yellowstone. Ordinarily sure-footed, animals sometimes venture too close to geyser basins, fall through the thin ground and die.
Photo by Jeff Foott / Panoramic Images

History

From the park's establishment until 1972, wildfires were aggressively suppressed, but from the early 1970s to the present, natural fire has been recognized as an important factor contributing to the health and biological diversity of the forest. Fires that do not threaten human life or property, are now monitored, but allowed to burn.

Yellowstone's Northern Range and wild ungulates were managed in the 1950s and 1960s with artificial reduction programs. In recent decades, range and wildlife managers have opted for natural regulation. Elk, bison and other herbivore populations are allowed to fluctuate in response to weather, predation, disease, aging, range conditions, and influences beyond the park boundaries.

In the 1970s, managers sought to make park resources available to winter visitors by permitting the use of over snow vehicles. At the turn of the century, snowmobile use became a controversial and divisive issue.

Park facilities had been deteriorating for decades due to insufficient maintenance and construction funding. Prior to 1994, no entry funds were retained specifically for use in Yellowstone. In 1994, Yellowstone was authorized to increase its entry fees and retain more than half for park projects. Projects being funded, in part, by this new program include renovation of visitor education centers, development of new exhibits, campground and amphitheater upgrades, scientific studies of bison, as well as research and preservation work. However large or small, each event, is recorded for posterity in the archives of Yellowstone, the scientific literature, public media, and private memories of the park's shareholders.

In 1972, at age 100, Yellowstone became America's first United Nations World Biosphere Reserve, in recognition of its great geological and biological significance and its importance as a major world ecosystem. There are now 209 international biosphere reserves in 55 countries, each, like Yellowstone, helping to maintain genetic diversity in an increasingly uniform and synthetic world.

Yellowstone was designated a UNESCO World Heritage site in 1978, adding to its international recognition. Yellowstone joined the august company of the Galapagos Islands, the Great Pyramids of Giza, Mount Kilimanjaro, the Great Barrier Reef, the Neolithic Flint Mines at Spiennes, Lake Baikal, Stonehenge, the Great Wall of China, and 746 other world treasures.

Yellowstone represents a major change in the relationship of people to the land, the evolution of an ecological conscience. It is a place, an ecosystem, and an idea that has since spread throughout the world. Yellowstone has been the model for parks and equivalent preserves in 134 countries, and the precursor to the system of more than 3,600 parks, world biosphere reserves, and world heritage sites established to preserve elements of our international human heritage on this fragile planet.

The legacy of Yellowstone in the United States is diverse. While the National Park System continues to

Above left: The Fishing Bridge was built in 1937. The original rough-hewn corduroy log bridge was built in 1902. For several decades the bridge was a very popular place to fish for the spawning cutthroat trout moving out of Yellowstone Lake. Fishing from this area was closed in 1973.
Photo by Jeff Henry

Above: The abundance of wildlife in Yellowstone will bring the visitor to many close-up situations with bison and many other species. It is imperative that safe distances be kept at all times.
Photo by Jeff Vanuga

Left: An angler makes a fly selection to try his luck on the wary trout of the firehole river. Yearly more than 75,000 fishermen wade the waters of the park in the quest for one of the local species of fish, especially the cutthroat trout. The park and its waters are considered by many fishermen as a "must" to fish in one's lifetime. Where else in the world can one fish for trophy trout within sight of bison and geysers?
Photo by John Juracek

grow, today there are 384 areas covering more than 83 million acres in 49 States, the District of Columbia, American Samoa, Guam, Puerto Rico, Saipan, and the Virgin Islands, there are numerous designations within the National Park System. The Congressional legislation authorizing the sites, or the President who proclaims them under authority of the Antiquities Act of 1906, name the areas. There are national parks, monuments, historic sites, historical parks, lakeshores, seashores, battlefields, recreation areas, trails, parkways, rivers, and even cemeteries, but others cannot be neatly categorized because of the diversity of resources within them. Some units of the National Park System bear unique titles or combination of titles, like the White House and Prince William Forest Park.

The National Park System encompasses approximately 83.6 million acres (339,000 km^2), of which more than 4.3 million acres (17,400 km^2) remain in private ownership. The largest area (Yellowstone once was) is Wrangell-St. Elias National Park and Preserve, in Alaska. At 13,200,000 acres (53,500 km^2) it represents 16.3 percent of the entire system.

The National Park Service, manned by a cadre of more than 14,000 permanent personnel and some 4,000 temporary seasonal personnel, serves about 270 million visitors each year. Specialists in such varied fields as scientific research, resources management, law enforcement, fire suppression, search and rescue, interpretation, maintenance, concessions management and administration comprise this proud, skilled, and professional organization. 75,000 volunteers in national parks and affiliated areas contributed $35 million worth of services in one year alone, from maintaining the Appalachian National Scenic Trail, to welcoming visitors at information desks, to monitoring vital biological research plots.

The mission of the National Park Service, stated in the Organic Act that created it in 1916 is " ... *to promote and regulate the use of the ...national parks...which purpose is to conserve the scenery and the natural and historic objects and the wildlife therein and to provide for the enjoyment of the same in such a manner and by such means as will leave them unimpaired for the enjoyment of future generations.*" In 1970, Congress elaborated on the 1916 National Park Service Organic Act, by adding that all units of the system have equal legal standing in a national system.

Above right: A few elk relax in front of a part of the historic Fort Yellowstone area and the park headquarters at Mammoth Hot Springs.
Photo by Raymond K. Gehman

Above: One of the largest wood structures in the world, the Old Faithful Inn features a majestic grand lobby. Made of lodgepole pine and detailed with burled pine the lobby is six-stories high.
Photo by Tom Murphy

Right: The Old Faithful Inn was built to reflect the surrounding marvels of Yellowstone and the Upper Geyser Basin, the materials used for its construction were collected in the park and included lodgepole pines, volcanic rocks for the fireplace and even obsidian sand as part of the concrete. The structure was commissioned in 1902 by commercial interests in the park and was designed by Robert C. Reamer, a 29-year-old architect who wished to build a structure to complement and fit within its surroundings. He also built the Grand Canyon Hotel and the Mammoth Hot Springs Hotel among others.
Photo by Mary Liz Austin

Yellowstone Quick Facts

Date Established:
- **Yellowstone National Park** (YNP) is the world's first national park.
- Established on March 1, 1872.
- Designated as America's first United Nations Biosphere Preserve in 1972.
- Designated a World Heritage Site in 1978.

Geography:
- 3,468 square miles (2,219,791 acres; 898,000 ha) with 96% in Wyoming, 3% in Montana, and 1% in Idaho. Larger than the states of Rhode Island and Delaware combined.
- Figure-eight Grand Loop Road carries travelers near important features of the park on 140-miles (225 km) of paved roads. About 1,000 miles (1,600 km) of trails criss-cross the park for a closer look.
- YNP is central to the 28,000 square miles (72,520 km^2) Greater Yellowstone Ecosystem.
- More than 20 peaks over 10,000 feet (3,048 m).
- Highest point: Eagle Peak, 11,358 feet (3,461 m).
- Lowest point: Reese Creek, 5,282 feet (1,609 m).
- Precipitation: From 10 to 80 inches (25-203 cm) annually depending on location.
- More than 5% of park covered by water, or about 173 square miles (448 km^2) with more than 500 streams and 150 lakes.
- There are about 275 waterfalls dropping 15 feet (4.5 m) or more; tallest being Lower Falls of the Yellowstone at 308 feet (94 m).
- Yellowstone Lake has 136 square miles (352 km^2) of surface area with more than 110 miles (177 km) of shoreline, has an average depth of 140 feet (43 m) and reaches 400 feet (123 m) at its deepest.
- The park includes headwater streams of the Missouri, Columbia and Colorado.
- Temperature averages 9°F (-13°C) in January to 80°F (27°C) in July depending on location. The weather is unpredictable, even during summer.

Geology:
- Yellowstone has one of the largest calderas in the world, 45 by 30 miles (72 x 48 km).
- There are more than 10,000 geothermal features including more than 300 geysers.
- World's tallest geyser, Steamboat Geyser, erupts sporadically 300 to 500 feet (91 to 152 m).
- The park harbors one of the largest petrified forests in the world.
- There are about 2,000 earthquakes a year in Yellowstone.

Fauna:
- 7 species of wild ungulates.
- 2 species of bears: grizzly and black.
- Wolves: successfully restored in 1995 and 1996, with a healthy and growing population.
- 50 species of other mammals.
- 311 species of birds observed in the park.
- 18 species of fish with 6 non-native species including a hybrid cutthroat/rainbow.
- 6 species of reptiles, 4 species of amphibians.
- 5 species within Yellowstone are threatened or endangered.
- Heat tolerant bacteria thrive in the hot waters of Yellowstone.

Flora:
- More than 1,700 native vascular plant species. Life zones separate the plants from semiarid grasslands to high alpine tundra.
- 8 species of conifers, lodgepole pine dominant.
- About 170 species of non-native plants.
- About 186 species of lichen are found.

General Information:
The park is open year-round. Some park roads are closed during winter. Entrance fees are collected. Pick up a free copy of the park's newspaper *Yellowstone Today*, with current information on road condition, closures, safety precautions, and general activities.

Park Headquarters: Located at Mammoth Hot Springs P.O. Box 168, YNP, WY 82190 (307-344-7381). Internet: www.nps.gov/yell with extended planning page at: www.nps.gov/yell/planvisit/

Park Information Centers: Visitor centers and contact stations in operation with rangers on duty and free information (check for seasonal schedule). They are located at: Albright Visitor Center and Museum: Open 365 Days at Mammoth Hot Springs, Old Faithful Visitor Center: Film, geyser eruptions prediction information, Canyon Visitor Center, Fishing Bridge Museum & Visitor Center, Grant Village Visitor Center, West Thumb Information Station, Norris Geyser Basin Museum and Museum of the National Park Ranger, and the Madison Information Station.

Camping: The park provides campsites on a first-come, first-served basis at different sites call 307-344-7381, or visit: www.nps.gov/yell

Accessibility: Accessible facilities in some areas, campsites, restrooms, and trails. A guidebook, "Visitors guide to Accessible Features in YNP," is available at the gates and information centers or write to: Park Accessibility Coordinator, P.O. Box 168, YNP, WY 82190 (307-344-2018).

Lodging and Other Services:
Xanterra Parks & Resorts: Provides lodging, dining, and some camping services in the park (307-344-7311 or 307-344-5566). www.Travel Yellowstone.com or www.xanterra.com

Delaware North Companies/Yellowstone General Stores: Provide convenience and gift shops in many areas of the park (406-586-7593). www.yellowstonestores.com

To Further Your Research:
National Park Service: Offers extended information on its website. www.nps.gov/yell Animals page and wolf population updates: www.nps.gov/ycll/nature/animals/ Additional information on geothermal features: www.nps.gov/yell/nature/geothermal/index.html; with great links.

Yellowstone Association: Non-profit; provides educational products and services to promote preservation of Yellowstone National Park since 1933. Operates 8 bookstores in the park and a website with online bookstore. Contact: P.O. Box 117, YNP, WY 82190 (304-344-2296). www.YellowstoneAssociation.org

Yellowstone Association Institute: Provides classes, seminars, and guided educational trips in the park (304-344-2294). Contact the Yellowstone Association.

To Help Yellowstone:

The Yellowstone Park Foundation: Private, non-profit organization dedicated to the protection, preservation and enhancement of the Park. Depends on private and corporate donations. 37 East Main, Suite 4. Bozeman, MT 59715 (406-586-6303). www.ypf.org

The Greater Yellowstone Coalition: Working to protect the GYE and to promote its understanding. P.O. Box 1874. Bozeman, MT 59771 (406-586-1593). www.greateryellowstone.org

All information valid as of press time. As information may be subject to change, please contact the National Park Service. Also check Elanpublishing.com for additional links, information and suggested reading list.

Above: Old Faithful Inn on a foggy cold morning.
Photo by Mary Liz Austin

Right: Tower Fall and rainbow. Tower Creek plunges 132 feet (40 m) at this beautiful waterfall before meeting with the Yellowstone River.
Photo by Jeff Gnass

Back Cover: Old Faithful Geyser is the world's most popular Geyser. The eruption lengths and the intervals between eruptions vary. A geyser prediction chart is posted at the Old Faithful Visitor Center. The height of the eruptions average at about 145 feet (44 m) with small ones just above 100 feet (30 m) and large ones up to 185 feet (56 m).
Photo by Larry Ulrich